LISTENING
IS *an* ACT
of LOVE

THE PENGUIN PRESS

New York

2007

LISTENING IS an ACT of LOVE

· · · · · · · ·

A Celebration of American Life
from the StoryCorps Project

· · · · · · · ·

Edited and with an Introduction by

DAVE ISAY

THE PENGUIN PRESS
Published by the Penguin Group
Penguin Group (USA) Inc., 375 Hudson Street, New York, New York 10014, U.S.A.
• Penguin Group (Canada), 90 Eglinton Avenue East, Suite 700, Toronto, Ontario,
Canada M4P 2Y3 (a division of Pearson Penguin Canada Inc.) • Penguin Books Ltd,
80 Strand, London WC2R 0RL, England • Penguin Ireland, 25 St Stephen's Green,
Dublin 2, Ireland (a division of Penguin Books Ltd) • Penguin Books Australia Ltd,
250 Camberwell Road, Camberwell, Victoria 3124, Australia (a division of Pearson
Australia Group Pty Ltd) • Penguin Books India Pvt Ltd, 11 Community Centre,
Panchsheel Park, New Delhi – 110 017, India • Penguin Group (NZ), 67 Apollo Drive,
Rosedale, North Shore 0632, New Zealand (a division of Pearson New Zealand Ltd.)
• Penguin Books (South Africa) (Pty) Ltd, 24 Sturdee Avenue, Rosebank,
Johannesburg 2196, South Africa

Penguin Books Ltd, Registered Offices:
80 Strand, London WC2R 0RL, England

First published in 2007 by The Penguin Press,
a member of Penguin Group (USA) Inc.

Copyright © Sound Portraits Productions, Inc., 2007
All rights reserved

Photo credits: pp. 2, 4, 204—Christopher Weil, Chris Weil Photography; p. 253—Russ
Berkman, Russ Berkman Photography; p. 289—Brett Myers, StoryCorps; all other
photographs are property of Sound Portraits Productions, Inc.

Library of Congress Cataloging-in-Publication Data

Listening is an act of love : a celebration of American lives from the StoryCorps Project
/ edited and with an introduction by Dave Isay.
p. cm.
ISBN-13: 978-1-59420-140-0
1. United States—Social life and customs—1945–1970—Anecdotes.
2. United States—Social life and customs—1971—Anecdotes.
3. United States—History—1945—Anecdotes. 4. National characteristics,
American—Anecdotes. 5. United States—Biography—Anecdotes. 6. Interviews—
United States. 7. Oral history. 8. StoryCorps (Project)
I. Isay, David. II. StoryCorps (Project)

Printed in the United States of America
1 3 5 7 9 10 8 6 4 2

DESIGNED BY AMANDA DEWEY

This book is dedicated to the ten thousand pairs of participants—
and counting—who have borne out our motto
time and time again:

Listening is an act of love

CONTENTS

The essence of America lies not in the headlined heroes . . .
but in the everyday folks who live and die unknown,
yet leave their dreams as legacies.

— ALAN LOMAX, 1940

LISTENING
IS *an* ACT
of LOVE

INTRODUCTION

StoryCorps is built on a few basic ideas:

That *our* stories—the stories of everyday people—are as interesting and important as the celebrity stories we're bombarded with by the media every minute of the day.

That if we take the time to listen, we'll find wisdom, wonder, and poetry in the lives and stories of the people all around us.

That we all want to know our lives have mattered and we won't ever be forgotten.

That listening is an act of love.

Participating in StoryCorps is a simple process. First, you make an appointment to visit one of our recording booths. Bring anyone you choose—your grandmother, your dad, your

StoryCorps booth in Grand Central Terminal

sister, your best friend, the waitress at the local diner whose story you've always been curious about. A trained StoryCorps facilitator will greet you, take you into the booth, and shut the door.

Inside, the booth is completely silent. The lights are low. The room is cozy. You sit at a small table across from, let's say, your grandmother, looking into her eyes. There's a microphone in front of each of you. The facilitator sits down in front of an audio console and presses *Record*. You begin to ask your questions:

"What are the most important lessons you've learned in life?"

"What did your mother sing to you when you were a baby?"

"How do you want to be remembered?"

At the end of forty minutes, two broadcast-quality CDs have been created. One goes home with you. A second becomes part of an archive at the American Folklife Center at the Library of Congress so that your great-great-grandchildren will someday be able to listen to the voices of you and your grandmother. Excerpts of interviews are broadcast each Friday on NPR's *Morning Edition*.

StoryCorps launched on October 23, 2003, in New York's Grand Central Terminal. The great oral historian Studs Terkel, who was ninety-one at the time, flew in from Chicago to cut the ribbon. "Today we shall begin celebrating the lives of the uncelebrated!" he proclaimed. "We're in Grand Central Station. We know there was an architect, but who hung the iron? Who were the brick masons? Who swept the floors? These are the noncelebrated people of our country. In this booth the noncelebrated will speak of their lives. It might be a grandmother speaking to a grandchild. It might be a kid talking to his uncle. It might be a neighbor talking to a neighbor. And suddenly they will realize that they are the ones who have built this country!"

Since that day we've added another permanent booth at Ground Zero and launched three mobile recording studios that travel the country year-round gathering stories. Each session represents an act of love and respect: forty minutes set aside to ask important questions and listen closely to the answers. The interviews honor our families, friends, and elders: the ordinary people we find all around us who, in their day-to-day acts of

kindness, courage, and humanity, embody the true spirit of our nation.

StoryCorps is a project about permanence in an ever more disposable society. It reminds us of what's really important in the midst of all of life's distractions. It encourages us to connect despite endless temptations to detach and disengage.

On the following pages are forty-nine stories selected from the ten thousand interviews we've recorded to date. We consider each StoryCorps session sacred, and we place great value on every story that's been recorded as part of the project. It is a joy and an honor for all of us at StoryCorps to do this work, and it's a privilege to share these stories with you.

. . .

4

AUTHOR'S NOTE

The following stories were edited from transcripts of forty-minute StoryCorps interviews. We aimed to distill these stories without altering the tone or meaning of the original sessions. Words and phrases that read well are not always the best spoken moments, and the reverse is also the case. As a result, the phrasings of the same story in print and in audio may vary slightly.

We did not use ellipses to indicate omitted text; at times tense and usage were changed for clarity. Each story was fact-checked. Participants gave permission for edited versions of their interviews to be published in this book. A few participants requested that their ages not be included, and we honored that request.

HOME

and

FAMILY

When StoryCorps launched, I wasn't sure whether the interviews would resonate with anyone other than the participants and their families. I also suspected that we'd start hearing the same stories repeated over and over again.

From the day we opened, I was taken by the power and universality of the recordings coming out of the booth. Most StoryCorps interviews revolve around the three great themes of human existence—birth, love, and death—but from these themes emerge an astonishing array of stories.

One day, about a year into the project, the senior producer for StoryCorps, Sarah Kramer, came up to me and said, "You know, the longer the project runs, the better the stories seem to get." Her words remain true to this day.

CYNTHIA RAHN, 48, interviewed by her friend ADRIENNE LEA, 47

RECORDED IN DURHAM, NORTH CAROLINA

Cynthia Rahn: I lived very far out in the country, and I had just started kindergarten with a lot of kids from town that I didn't know. We had an assignment to bring in either a toy or a stuffed animal or something you found in your barn so that we could create a barnyard diorama. I was a little shy and insecure because I knew I was from out in the country and probably looked poor to everybody else, and certainly everybody else looked rich to me. So I felt a little intimidated.

But Mrs. White was a wonderful lady. Very loving and considerate. When she gave us the assignment, she made it very exciting. And I don't think she had a clue that completing the assignment would be a problem for anyone. She said, "Go home, find something that has to do with a farm animal or a barn, and bring it in tomorrow, and we'll all as a group create a farmyard scene here at kindergarten." We were very excited about it when we left to go home. But once I got home, I took off my school clothes and ran outside to play. I completely forgot about the assignment, and played until dark.

When my mother got home from work, we came in and ate and got ready to go to bed. And then I realized I had forgotten to do anything to prepare for this assignment. And so, here was Momma, just got home from work, tired, and I said, "Oh my gosh, I've got to get a cow or a hoe or a stuffed animal," something that represents a farm. We looked, and I did not have one single farmyard toy. I didn't have a plastic horse. I didn't have a stuffed cow. We had nothing. So it was dark, and it was time to go to bed. And I started to cry. I got really upset. And I said, "I can't go to school tomorrow and not have anything." And Momma said, "It's too late. There's no stores open." In rural Appalachia there were no Wal-Marts; you couldn't just ride out and get something. And so, in addition to getting upset, I started to get a little angry because I felt my momma wasn't helping me. She said, "Well, you should have thought about this when you got home. You waited too late. You weren't responsible. You have to go to bed now."

I went to bed upset and angry, and then next morning I got up and the first thing I thought of, laying in my bed, was "I don't have anything to take to school." Momma worked, so she had to leave early. She left before we got up, and she would leave us breakfast.

I went downstairs, and sitting on the kitchen table was a barn made out of notebook paper. She had just taken plain notebook paper and folded it; and she folded the walls, she folded the roof, she folded the doors that opened so horses could go in and out. She had shutters on the windows. She had little steps that went up to the loft. And it was just sitting there. It was like magic. I looked at it—there wasn't a staple in it. There was no tape. She had just folded a barn for me.

I was so happy and so excited when I saw that barn. I was like, "I can't believe she did that!" My sister took me to kindergarten. And when I came in, the other kids had bags of store-bought plastic farm animals. And everybody was so amazed at my barn. I felt like the most special kid in the class. My mother is not the origami type, so I have no idea where she learned to do that. I have no idea how long that would have taken her to do or how she figured out how to make that barn.

It made me a very happy little girl, and I was very popular that day in school. I just felt like a queen. And I knew, too, that she cared.

April 13, 2006

. . . .

DR. RICHARD COLLINS, 81, interviewed by his grandson SEAN COLLINS, 26

RECORDED IN NEW YORK CITY

Richard Collins: I was born in Avon, New York, in 1924, one of twelve children. My father was a country doctor, and it was my father's job when he made calls to take three or four of us in the car with him, to get us out of my mother's hair. When we would arrive at a house to make a call, we were forbidden to leave the car, and we were forbidden to blow the horn unless one of us was dying. So we were pretty constrained.

One time I was in the car with my brother Chuck, and my father was delivering a baby. And the time wore on. We were getting pretty bored, so we started exploring his pill case. We started looking at the different colored pills. Then we smelled them. Finally, we tasted them. And we came across ones that tasted like licorice. So we chewed them up. He was smaller than I, so I gave him less than I took. And it turned out that they were something called Evac-U-Gen, which was a laxative. And by the time my father came out from his call, we had thoroughly fouled the car, which taught my father a great lesson—and us as well.

When I was about fifteen, my father was working night and day, and I used to drive for him. It was a small town, and the constable used to turn his head when he'd see me driving my father down the street, knowing I didn't have a license. My mother used to wake me up at night to drive him for his night calls. And one night in the wintertime we went up to a farmhouse. I came as close to the farmhouse as I could, but because of the snow it was difficult. I left the headlights on so that he could see his way. And just as he got closer to the farmhouse, the biggest, blackest dog that I ever saw came tearing around the corner of the barn and just took a leap at him. I was terrified, and I was too far away to do anything. But without hesitation my father swirled the bag up and hit that dog under the jaw, and the dog went howling back around the barn. When he got back from the call, I said, "Dad, I was so scared! I was afraid that dog was going to get you!" And he said, "Always remember one thing, Dick: Never hit the dog until he's got all four feet off of the ground." Good advice.

Sean Collins: What about school?

Richard: At Saint Agnes Parochial School in the mornings, Sister Edmunda used to have a little toady who would ring a bell. Anybody who came in after that bell was late and got a demerit. And that was a chronic problem I had, getting up a little late. So I grew to hate that bell. One day I left the lock on the school window open. Later on, I stole back to the school, went in the window, and stole that bell. The next day there was hell to pay because somebody had taken that bell. Sister said it was a sin against the school; it was a sin against the Sisters, a sin against the faith, a sin against the Pope. And I knew it was such a terrible sin that there was no way I could bring the shame on my family to confess to that. So I kept it locked in my heart over all those years. And, of course, Sisters came and Sisters went. Popes came and Popes went. And I still had that sin locked in my heart.

Sean: What did you end up doing with the school bell?

Richard: I still have it. It's by my bedside, and I joyfully ring it every now and then.

I was just thinking, by the way, of my first-grade teacher, a saintly nun named Sister Monica. I eventually became her physician. She was in her eighties, still teaching but running out of gas. And she would come to my office, and I would give her shots of vitamin B_{12} and anything else I could think of, but nothing was working. So finally I hit upon a solution. I wrote her a prescription for a *spiritus fermenti*, which is Latin for "fermented spirits." And she would take the prescription down to the drugstore, and the druggist would pour from the bottle of Schenley's into a medicine bottle. She would take two tablespoons before breakfast and two before lunch. It worked like a charm. But if she had ever come on the truth of the matter, I'm sure she would have excommunicated me from the faith.

Sean: Would you mind telling me a little bit about how you met my grandmother?

Richard: No, because she's the absolute light of my life. She came to Avon when I was a sophomore in high school. She was and is a beautiful redhead, and she just grabbed my heart—although during high school we didn't get along very well. I went out of my way to do little things so that she wouldn't forget me. But they were always the wrong things, and they got me in trouble. I can remember one time we were in a school play called *Dollars for Doughnuts*. She was the older girl, and I was her bratty brother. And there was one scene in the play where she was supposed to complain of being faint, and I was supposed to go up and get a little vase of water that had some flowers in it and sprinkle it on her. So, before the play, I thought, "I'm going to look around school and see if I can't find a big vase." So I found a gigantic vase and put a few pussy willows in it and filled it up to the brim with water and put it on the piano. It must have been a gallon and a half of cold water. And she had a brown taffeta dress on, I remember. And in the middle of the play she said, "Oh! I feel faint!" So I marched up to the piano, and I threw out the pussy willows, and I dumped the bucket of water on her. And she looked at me for about thirty seconds, and then she brought one right up from the floor, whacked me across the face, and almost took my head off. I have a condition called dermatographia, where my skin swells if you scratch it very much, so the whole left side of my face went up for the rest of the play. And to this day the people in Avon say they've never seen such acting as took place on that stage that day.

Sean: So how'd you go from there?

Richard: With patience and persistence and timing. I never dated her until I graduated from high school. And then it was a long-distance relationship, because I went off to college and medical school. But it worked. And she's been the light of my life ever since. A wonderful woman.

Yeah. I've had a good life. Although there are things that we would all do differently if we had the chance, I don't think there are any huge regrets. But I'll have to say that out of all of this I had the great good fortune of meeting your grandma. That just changed my whole life. And it's been such a great source of wonder and help to me. So if I'm going to give you any advice, it's to get yourself a pretty redhead like your grandma!

September 24, 2005

SETH FLEISCHAUER, 25, interviews his grandfather WILLIAM JACOBS, 83

RECORDED IN NEW YORK CITY

William Jacobs remembers a visit from his future mother-in-law while he was recuperating from a car accident during World War II.

William Jacobs: A nurse came into my room and she said, "Lieutenant, you have a visitor." And I said, "Who's that?" And she said, "A Mrs. Gropper." Gropper was Claire's last name, so I thought she must have misunderstood Miss for Mrs. So I said, "Is she an old lady or young?" And she said, "Well, I guess I would call her old." And I said, "Well, tell her to come in." And in comes Claire's mother.

She said, "Billy, I have to tell you some things. I heard Claire on the telephone last night saying how happy she was, and she's talking about how you're going to have babies and so on and so forth. I have to tell you something." I said, "What is that, Mrs. Gropper?" And she said, "Claire cannot have children." And she went on to give me some details of how when Claire was five years old, she was in the hospital and some doctor had erred rather severely. She never made Claire aware of this, and she wanted me to know this, and wanted to know if I was willing to marry her anyhow.

I said, "Yes, Mrs. Gropper, I am ready to marry her anyhow." And she took a deep breath and she said, "Billy, I want to ask you something else. Will you be willing to adopt children? Because I know Claire would love to have children." And I said, "Yes, Mrs. Gropper, I would be glad to adopt children, and I would do so." She was very relieved, and she said, "I only have one other question, Billy. How are we going to tell Claire?" And I said, "Mrs. Gropper, I will tell her myself on our wedding night." And that's what happened.

Seth Fleischauer: Throughout my life you've been a source of inspiration to me, and I think the biggest thing you did in my life was the dedication I saw you give to Grandma in those last seven or eight years that she had Alzheimer's. Seeing that example of true love and true dedication, especially for someone like me, a child of divorce, that's the biggest thing that you've brought to me in my life.

William: Thank you, Seth. I found it absolutely painless taking care of her, so I guess I did have true love for her. Never for a minute did I think, "God, when is this going to be over?" I never, ever thought that. In fact, I find that since she's died, I've kind of been floundering and trying to figure out what to do with the rest of my life. I find this period to be much more unsatisfactory than all of those years of caring for her. I just didn't find it that much of a burden at all.

Seth: I think that's what was so remarkable about it for me. Thank you very much for doing this, Grandpa. This was really great and unexpected. I know I'd heard these stories before, but in this setting it was very special.

William: Well, it was very special for me, Seth. I just loved doing it. And just looking at you and answering you, with your eyes looking into mine and mine into yours, it's just great.

Seth: I love you, Grandpa.

William: Thank you, Seth. I love you, too.

July 15, 2005

JOYCE KIM LEE, 35, interviews her mother, HEE-SOOK LEE, 66

RECORDED IN SANTA MONICA, CALIFORNIA

Joyce Kim Lee: My friends who have parents who are Korean immigrants, they've never actually seen their parents hug or kiss or show affection towards each other. So I think it's pretty unusual for a first-generation Korean couple to be so affectionate. Can you tell me where you learned this from?

Hee-Sook Lee: Yes, that is a very important story. When I started going to church, I met an American missionary couple. They were in their sixties at the time. (Of course, they are now both of them in heaven.) They started an English Bible class at their house with forty or fifty young college students. And as we sat there in the living room, we were not only learning the Bible, but we were observing their life together. When I see them, they always say, "Honey, I love you" and "Honey, thank you." And then when the wife bring some tea, he grab her arms and kiss her. And then when she started washing dishes, the husband was standing beside and drying. Wow, they are so happy, always smiling.

When it comes to my family, my mother, she served her husband, my dad, like a king. I never heard Dad say, "Thank you" or "I love you." Never heard that in all those years. So I decided, "When I get married, I want to be a happy, sweet couple like missionary friend."

So, of course, when I come to the United States, I get married to typical Korean husband. I said, "Honey, I love you." And typical man, just sitting in the living room and reading a newspaper, didn't respond. So I said again, "I love you," and he said, "Okay." And I wasn't satisfied with that answer. So I said, "I love you." And he said, "Oh, me, too." I said, "Can't you say 'I love you, too'?" And at first he said it was very hard. He's not used to expressing. So the next day, "I love you." He said, "Same here." So I said, "I love you," until he responded, "I love you, too." And later on it wasn't difficult. He just said, "I love you, too." And then, hug, even kiss on my cheek. A lot of Korean couples were amazed. "Wow, how wonderful your marriage!" And so that was the start. I determined I would have that kind of family: very sweet expressions of love, appreciation, happy, happy family, which now we have. You approve, right?

Joyce: Yes, I love it. Do you have any advice for young couples?

Hee-Sook: I practice three phrases to use a lot in your good, happy marriage. First, express to each other: "I love you, honey." The second phrase is "Thank you." A lot of times you just take for granted—for example, Dad takes all the garbage out. It's his job, but I always say, "Thank you, honey, for taking all the garbage out!" Every little thing, express your gratitude. And I cook all the time. He always say, "Thank you, honey, for your good cooking" and "I really enjoyed your meal! It was delicious!" You know, that kind of thing is very important. Appreciate each other. And the other thing is saying sorry: "I'm very sorry." Sometimes men make a mistake, and in men's pride they don't want to admit they made a mistake.

And a woman, they are sensitive to say, "I'm sorry." But we practice a lot. "Honey, I'm sorry. It was my mistake. I misunderstood." And then, "Okay."

Just say, "I'm sorry," and then you will overcome the crisis of the husband and wife fighting each other. When you say, "I'm sorry," that's the end of it.

January 21, 2006

. . . .

SULOCHANA KONUR, 53, interviewed by her daughter-in-law, MELISSA KONUR, 31

RECORDED IN NEW YORK CITY

Sulochana Konur: I was a biology student in my first year of college in India, and I was doing a dissection of a frog or some such thing, and my father sent for me. When I went home, there were lots of people around the house. My mom said I needed to wash my face and change my clothes. I knew better than to argue, so I just said, "Okay." And then I went into the room where my future mother-in-law, my future sister-in-law, and their friends were. There were about eight or nine ladies in the small room. And so I met with them and they talked to me, and they asked me questions like "What do you study in school?" They were simple questions.

Then the custom is that my mom makes some food, and I'm supposed to take that to the men in the living room. That's when the future husband-to-be gets to see you. And so I did. I went and passed the plate to everyone. There were seven or eight people, and my husband, and my husband's friend was there. The rest of them were older, so I knew one of the two had to be the groom-to-be, but I didn't know which one. So I just sat down, and my father asked me some questions and I answered.

After they left, I argued with my parents and I cried, and I said that I want to go to college, I want to be a doctor, I don't want to get married. And my father said, "They can always say no, so don't worry. I had to do this because a friend of mine suggested it. This was just a last-minute thing. The next time I won't agree to this." And so I said, "Okay!"

I didn't even think about it the second day. But about a week later my father got a letter saying that that family was interested. He didn't tell me that, but I heard my dad talking to my mom. So they went and visited the family, and they came back in the night, and I was awake. I remember hearing my father say to my mother that it's a good family. So I knew after that, that it was going to be the marriage. There was nothing I could do.

I was fifteen and eight months when I got married. We just now finished thirty-seven years together.

Melissa Konur: So how much longer did you stay in India before you came to the United States?

Sulochana: Three years after marriage. We landed in Tucson, Arizona, and I said, "There's so much space and no people!" That was my first impression of the United States. And then we collected our baggage and went to the car, and then the car was really tiny, so I said, "Here the cars are only meant for two people, not for fifteen people like India." And so I got in, and we started driving.

It was really, really wide roads—four lanes each way— beautiful, beautiful roads and lit, and we were the only car because this was like one o'clock in the middle of the night. So I said, "Why do they build such big streets and have such tiny cars and nobody around?" I think the shocking thing was that there were so many fewer people in this country—until I come to Manhattan.

Melissa: What was your first impression when Sanjay first brought me home? You can be honest. (*Laughter.*)

Sulochana: I didn't know how to feel. Confused, I would say. It wasn't natural, let's put it that way. Because I came from an arranged marriage. And even though I never thought that my children would go with a completely arranged marriage, I had imagined picking a girl for him and then introducing him to the girl—not him introducing me to the girl. So that was like a reversal, switching of the role.

Sanjay asked permission to bring you home, and we didn't know what we were supposed to do, because this is culturally different for us. But, you remember, we came to the airport, and you both walked off the airplane. In those days we could go up to the gate in the airport, so we were at the gate. And Sanjay— I felt Sanjay was more uncomfortable than I was. He said, "Mom, this is Melissa. Melissa, this is Mom and Dad." And so I remember giving you a hug and bringing you home. And since you were so talkative, it was easy. You were yourself, and hopefully I was myself, and so it didn't take us too long to like you.

I got into a marriage without knowing the person, but yet was committed to spend the rest of my life with the person. You both are good people, and we would like to see you both make this marriage work. But I don't think it's going to be different for you than it was for me, even though you have known Sanjay and this is your choice. If anything, it will be more difficult for you, because you have gone across the culture. There is no commonality other than the humanity.

Rather than look for what you have in common, you have to grow together. The only reason that marriages work is because you are friends and are respecting of each other.

October 1, 2005

VICTORIA KELLER FRASER, 58,
speaks with her grandson,
CHRISTOPHER JAMES FRASER, 20

RECORDED IN BURLINGTON, VERMONT

Christopher James Fraser: We're approaching the ten-year anniversary of my coming to live with you. My first question would be: What was your initial reaction ten years ago, almost on this date, to see a ten-year-old kid with a fair amount of sadness in him, and apparently not doing well, sitting in your kitchen with not so much as a phone call prior to that?

Victoria Keller Fraser: I walked in the door, and you were there unexpectedly. Grandpa was there. He told me that the police had called and that they had taken you away from your dad and that they had brought you here. I was surprised. I called SRS [the Department of Social and Rehabilitation Services], and they told me they were interested in placing you with us because your dad was arrested.

Is it all right with you if I say why he was arrested?

Christopher: Oh, yeah, that's fine.

Victoria: He was arrested for the possibility of having molested you. [He was later convicted.] Some people had witnessed something they were uncomfortable with and had called the police, and the police had come and taken you away from him. The state had been also trying to find your mother, who you were not supposed to be staying with because of your past history with her. [Christopher had been removed from his mother's custody at the age of six.] So the police came in the middle of the night and brought papers to us authenticating that the state wanted to have you in our household so that if your mother's attorney showed up at the door, he couldn't take you away. This was a few days before school started.

Christopher: Actually, I came to live with you the day before fourth grade started.

Victoria: You were very upset. You were very sad. You missed your dad just terribly. Fiercely. You had a toothbrush that belonged to your dad. That was the only thing that you had that was your dad's, and you— It was just really a cherished possession. Your grief was really big.

You were quite amazing. You've always been, but in that first month you were unusually amazing. The things that you would say to us. Do you remember when you came in—this was in the first few days—and you said, "I really don't think I ought to be living with you"? You came and told me that a couple of times, because you thought your mother could come and hurt us. And I talked to you about how I really didn't think that was going to happen. But that if she did come and if something bad did happen, that it wouldn't be your fault, and that I thought that you did need to be here. And then you came and talked to us about how we were "castle people" and you were a street person. Do you remember that?

Christopher: Yeah, I remember that. Yup.

Victoria: Because you had been homeless with your dad, which we also didn't really know about, and we had a nice home. So we talked about being castle and street people, and I didn't quite agree. I understood what you were saying, and I thought it was very perceptive of you to say that, but I also thought that you belonged with us. So you stayed.

Christopher: And you had a great vocabulary, and I talked like Rocky.

Victoria: Yeah, but your vocabulary grew enormously within two or three months. It was really amazing. You were ten years old. I'd really loved you before you came. But then after you came to live with us, I'd say to my friends, "This is an amazing person. Who is this?" Because I thought you comported yourself really extraordinarily.

It's been a lot of fun having you here with us. You're very funny, and you make wonderful comments. And you're kind and generous. And you're extremely compassionate. And being your grandmother allows me to have an arm's-length perspective. When you're a parent, you have more of a vested interest, but because I'm your grandmother, I'm sort of at arm's length.

Christopher: That's interesting, because one of the questions we wanted to discuss is that you never had a child of your own.

Victoria: Because I'm a step-grandmother. But I've been in your life your whole life, so I consider myself your grandmother.

Christopher: You've been there the whole time. Then ten years ago you took over what my parents should have been doing—playing both roles. You have the grandmother role, but your arm's length came in a little. It's interesting, because I actually feel kind of— There's one thing I feel kind of sad about. It's that I haven't ever really taken the time to give you direct praise. I can say it to anyone else, but I sometimes find it hard to say directly to you. But one thing that I've always admired is you have this ridiculous plate that you handle. It's almost a buffet. It's just constant. It's like you're the epicenter. At this point you're the caretaker for Grandpa in his transition of passing away. Your ability to devote your energy to so many things, and you do it in almost— To say it's graceful is a gross understatement, but you do it with an enthusiasm and optimism and just complete devotion.

Victoria: I brought this quote from Martha Washington. We don't hear too much about her, but I think this is a great quote. She said, "I am still determined to be cheerful and happy in whatever situation I may be, for I have also learned from experience that the greater part of our happiness or misery depends upon our dispositions and not upon our circumstances." So that's very much, I think, about being in the moment and just accepting what's happening.

Christopher: You're a miracle worker in so many different fashions. I have someone who I know I can go to, I know I can talk to. I never had that. So I guess, with all of your grace, you've managed to actually fill those gaps. You managed to make the pain a lot less. It's quite something. And it's a privilege to know somebody who has that capacity to be loving and caring, and be stern and solid when they need to be. Just as an example on how to lead one's life. So that'll have to be a big point in your biography if anyone should ever write it. "This is Victoria Fraser. She has the capacity to carry the world on her shoulders and run at the same time." I don't know too many people that can do that.

Victoria: Well, thank you. That's very kind of you to say.

August 11, 2006

· · · · · · · · · · ·

BRAD SKOW, 28, interviews
MARY LOU MAHER, 46, his birth mother

RECORDED IN NEW YORK CITY

Mary Lou Maher: I got pregnant when I was seventeen years old. It was my first year at Columbia University. I thought this child should be part of a complete family instead of just a mother with no father and someone who really wasn't old enough to have a baby.

So I sort of had this plan in my head. I wouldn't tell Mom and Dad, and I'd call up these people who I used to babysit for and see if I could live with them in California until the baby was born. They said that was fine. It was December when I found out I was pregnant. We organized that I would go out as soon as I finished the semester in May. I would stay at their place, and they had found someone who would adopt the child. And then that's what I did.

Brad Skow: So you didn't tell your parents?

Mary Lou: I didn't tell my parents. I'm kind of small, and I didn't look very pregnant.

My mom came to pick me up at the end of the semester. The plan was I'd spend one night at home and the next day I'd fly to California. They thought I was just going for a holiday.

My mom walked in the door, and she looked at me, and she said, "You're pregnant." And I said, "No, I'm not." And she goes, "Yes, you are. You're pregnant."

And that's how they found out. She took me home and gave me a really hard time—first of all about getting pregnant, and second about planning this whole adoption thing without telling them. They didn't want me to give up the baby. They did yell at me a lot, and I was very sad.

I told Conrad immediately, as soon as I heard from the doctor, so he knew from the beginning. He never talked about it even though we stayed together as boyfriend and girlfriend until I left for California in May. He just pretended I was away for the summer. Later on I heard his mother was very worried about him, and he was very depressed. He never went out of his room. And she kept trying to tell him that he could tell her anything, and she kept saying, "Nothing can't be solved except death. And if it's not death, then you should tell me." And he wouldn't.

I used to talk to you a lot when I was pregnant and explain the whole situation. I told you many times why I had to do this and that the best way to understand it was that I was taking care of you until the parents could get there. I wasn't ready to be a mother. I didn't have a father for you.

When the hard labor started, it was really hard. And then you were born, and it was really kind of cool to feel that relief after the baby comes out. And the doctor took you away quickly because I was afraid if I held you, I wouldn't be able to give you up. And then David arrived, my brother, who is a priest, and said he'd seen you, just so I'd know.

I remember after you were born, I was crying a lot, and one of the nurses came up and she hugged me for a really long time.

And she said, "It's going to be okay. It just takes time." Your parents picked you up the next morning. I left the same day. I was really sure this was the best decision.

The hardest part was when the adoption agency called me and said that they'd interviewed your parents, and they had some concerns about them as adopting parents because they didn't seem to get along very well and bickered. They asked me what I would do if they didn't approve the couple as adopting parents. And the answer was easy—I said I would come out and get you, and the adoption would be off. And then the adoption agency called back a couple days later and said they were approved. And that was kind of sad. It took about five years before I stopped thinking about you every day and crying, to just thinking about you every week, to the point where it only happened about once a month.

Brad: I was wondering if you could tell me about the moment when you first found out that I was searching for you.

Mary Lou: I was in the shower. I didn't hear the phone ring. My husband took the call. He came into the bathroom and said, "Conrad just called to tell you that he's heard from your son." I said, "Okay." He walked out and I cried. I took a really long shower. I was really, really sad and really, really happy and just anxious to talk to you. And then I got your phone number. I was excited. You weren't in your dorm, and I had to keep trying. You called me back when you got home from dinner. You sounded like a really interesting person. All I remember is I wanted you to just keep talking. I wanted to hear more. I wanted to know as much as possible.

Brad: So knowing what you know now, would you do it again?

Mary Lou: Knowing what I know now, I wouldn't do it again. The separation and the loss is just way too hard. We have a relationship now, and you're part of the family. But that feeling of having missed twenty years—you can't ever get that back.

November 23, 2004

. . . .

Cousins CHERIE JOHNSON, 72, and JAMES RANSOM remember visits to their grandmother's home in Bradenton, Florida

RECORDED IN SARASOTA, FLORIDA

James Ransom: I want to remind you about a lady named Miss Lizzie Devine. Miss Devine was a lady I thought was an apparition. She was a wiry lady. She wore summer dresses. She had a bandana and a straw hat. And she was the only person I knew who had more power than my grandmother. Grandma Minnie was a true matriarch, but everybody was in awe of Miss Devine.

Cherie Johnson: Miss Devine, when she braided your hair, your eyes went up in your head. You'd have to sleep on two soft pillows because she had your hair so tight. Miss Devine was a person that would put the fear of God into you. She wasn't a mean person, but she was stern. And when she said something, she meant exactly what she said.

James: She would come in on Sunday mornings and take us to Sunday school. And I didn't want to go to Sunday school with Miss Devine. When I saw her come down the road, Cherie, I thought that the leaves would be blowing off the trees and the sky would go black! I was afraid of her.

She came in the house one morning and said, "Children! Good morning, children!" And everybody, from my mother on down, said, "Good morning, Miss Devine." And she said, "It's time to go to Sunday school this morning, children!" And

I said, "Miss Devine, I can't go to Sunday school today." She said, "No?" I said, "No, ma'am." And she said, "Why not?" I said, "My mother didn't bring enough clothes for me to go to Sunday school this morning." She said, "Oh no?" I said, "No, ma'am." She said, "What kind of clothes do you have?" And I said, "All I have, Miss Devine, are my pajamas and my tennis shoes." She said, "That's okay, honey. Put your tennis shoes on. We'll go to Sunday school." I looked at Mother, and she looked *away. (Laughs.)* Miss Devine made me walk two blocks in my pajamas and my tennis shoes. I had to sit in church with my friends during Sunday school in my pajamas and my tennis shoes. I'll tell you, Cherie, I never lied again.

January 12, 2006

KAREN WASHABAU, 59, tells her husband, DAVE WASHABAU, 59, about her favorite aunt

RECORDED IN FLAGSTAFF, ARIZONA

Karen Washabau: I'd like to dedicate this conversation to my late aunt, my father's older sister. She was born in Altoona, Pennsylvania, in 1910 and lived in Altoona her whole life. Even though my grandparents didn't have any formal education beyond high school, they wanted their kids to get an education. So my aunt and my dad went away to college. She became a history teacher, and she taught eighth-grade history at Keith Junior High School in Altoona, Pennsylvania, for her whole career. She retired in 1970.

Aunt Mary never married, so the only kids that were really important to her were my brothers and me. Her name was Mary Elizabeth Ford, but I couldn't say "Aunt Mary" when I was tiny, so my mom said, "Well, why don't you call her 'Mef'?" That stands for her initials, Mary Elizabeth Ford. So I called her Mef all my life. My dad died when I was seventeen, very unexpectedly, and my mother was thrust into the role of being the sole parent to three kids. Luckily, we had Mef there to help us along.

She was only about five feet tall, probably never weighed more than 105 pounds, and was very neat. She lived a really independent life. She was not afraid to tackle anything. She traveled all over the world on a teacher's salary.

She loved politics and current events. When Kennedy and Nixon were running for president in 1960, the rumor around our neighborhood was that you didn't want to vote for Kennedy, because Kennedy was going to make everybody become Catholic. And I remember telling this to Mef, and she sat me down and whipped out her copy of an old history book with the Constitution and the Bill of Rights in it, and she had me read that. She said, "Do you think there's any way in the world that any president could make anybody become a certain religion?" And I had to take a step back and realize how ridiculous that was.

She never had anything bad to say about anybody, and she was always there for us. She was always there at plays and concerts and anything we were involved in. She loved to cook. She had a tiny house, a very small kitchen, and a stove that was half the size of a normal stove. But she could whip out just incredible meals. When I think of her, I see her in her little kitchen, bustling around, cooking. She's got an apron on, a bib apron, so that her clean, neat clothes would not get food on them. And there's always a Pirates game on the radio in the background. The Pittsburgh Pirates were like the soundtrack to her life. And she'd always be talking back to the announcer. Bob Prince was the play-by-play announcer back in those days, and she'd say things like "Oh, Prince, shut up!" or "Oh, Prince, go check your facts!"

I think of the holiday rituals, how she'd wrap up little things for stockings—little, tiny things that maybe weren't worth more than a dime, but she'd wrap them up meticulously so you'd have something to open. She started this notion of what she called a "lilly present." That's where you give somebody a gift for no reason at all. It's not Christmas, not their birthday—you just want to give them a gift. Every once in a while when I give you a gift unexpectedly, you're getting a "lilly present."

She always would force me to reexamine decisions that she could sense were maybe not the best decisions for me. When I was just a freshman in college, I became infatuated with a piano player from Long Island who was a little bit older. He wanted to elope, and one of the things that was so attractive was that his dad was a jeweler, and he would fit me up with a beautiful engagement ring. My mother's reaction was outrage. And Mary just sat me down and said, "What do you know about this man? Do you know his family? Does he want to be a father?" So I didn't run away and get married.

A second way that she really helped me was to always see that even in the worst situation there are bright spots on the horizon. I was finally engaged to a young man in my junior year of college. He broke off the engagement, and I was devastated. I came home for the weekend, and I was inconsolable. A day or two after I went back to school, I got a letter from Mef, and here are just a couple of lines from that letter:

> Dear Karen,
> You have loved a fine man, and this experience has enriched your life. Now you are going through a stormy period,

but storms pass. You have great strength, inherited from both your dad and your mother. Not the same kinds of strength, but the combination as found in you will be very good at sustaining you. Whatever you do, keep busy, and don't fret. Many things in life we can't understand, but we make the best of the situation and come out on top.

This letter is kind of worn and torn, and it's a testimony to how many times I looked at that letter in the course of my life.

I'd have to say probably the most wonderful thing she gave me, in addition to strength of character, was 450 to 500 letters that I wrote her, which she saved for me. We found these 500 letters when we were cleaning out her house. They were stuffed in the back of a little cupboard. And those letters really gave me back my own impressions of life. I never kept a diary in high school. Instead, I just wrote letters to Mef—and I knew she would never divulge them. So starting in seventh grade she got a litany of letters. Here's one that is an example of me in my early high school years. I say,

> *Dear Mef,*
> *I just had the final fight I'm ever going to have with Louis on Thursday. He said in school that I had rotten guts, and that I'd make a good pork chop. I came home and was so upset, but Mother showed me a letter that just came from Barry* [and Barry was a guy I'd had a crush on in sixth grade] *and well, Mef, Thursday turned out to be a wonderful day.*

There's not anybody that you would confess to that somebody said you had rotten guts, but I felt so comfortable with Mef that I shared that with her.

All her life the most important thing to her was being devoted to my brothers and me as an aunt. In a letter I wrote to her back in 1962, I was complaining about boys again. At the end of the letter I say, "You know I am so mad, I could just cry. So there you are. But then, what are aunts for?"

I mailed that on a Wednesday, and the next Monday she writes me a response. She says,

> *Dear Karen,*
>
> *Enclosed is a prompt answer to your question, "What are aunts for?" Well, I found this quote years ago in a book called* Mrs. Miniver, *and here's what I think aunts are for. "Aunts are to be a pattern and example to all aunts; to be a delight to boys (and girls) and a comfort to their parents; and to show that at least one daughter in every generation ought to remain unmarried, and raise the profession of auntship to a fine art." Thank you, Karen, for reminding me of this. I shall have to keep trying again and again to live up to it.*

And I would have to say that she not only raised auntship to that high art but that Mef was probably the gold standard. And I'm just very grateful that she was a part of my life.

March 20, 2006

ANTHONY D'ANDREA, 63, interviewed by his daughters MONICA MCINERNEY, 36, and MARY D'ANDREA, 35

RECORDED IN NEW YORK CITY

Anthony D'Andrea: I was born on August 24, 1930, and my mother said the church bells were ringing.

As a youngster I lived my entire life in the Bronx. The section I grew up in is called Highbridge, on 170th Street and Shakespeare Avenue. It was a great outlet for me as a boy, playing stickball in the street and a game called Sewers, where you throw the ball at the sewer and the other guys had to catch it. The big game was called Off the Point. We'd all chip together two cents here, three cents there and buy a "spaldeen," a pinkish-looking rubber ball. And you'd run up and you'd throw the ball and try to hit the molding on the apartment building. If you hit it right, it'd send the ball to the other side of the street. It was a big game. We'd have people watching us, and people with cars wouldn't want to park near us.

My dad came here from Italy in 1911, and he honestly believed that he could pick gold off the streets. My father would tell me who the Italian players were on the Yankees. And they had some great ones. Tony Lazzeri, Frank Crosetti, Joe DiMaggio, for example. And so I just developed a big interest in the Yankees.

Yankee Stadium was 161st Street and River Avenue, and that would be about a twenty- to twenty-five-minute walk up and down some pretty steep hills. I rarely went to a ball game, because we never had any money to do that. But when I was eleven or twelve, I used to go down in the morning when the Yankees were home to get autographs.

You could spot the players readily for two reasons, one of which was all the Yankee players had to wear jackets, ties, shirts. And the second reason is for twenty-five cents you got a book called *Who's Who in Baseball* with pictures of the team. It would come out just before the season started. Might've been twenty-five kids hanging around, and we'd wait by the subway stop. There's the elevated subway line, and they all exited pretty much at the same spot, so you could see them coming readily.

I was such an avid fan. On one occasion I found a ball on the street, and I started getting different players to sign it. My father used to get the *Daily News* every morning, and there was always a story about the Yankees. Whether they won or lost or if they weren't playing, there'd be a story. And this one day I noticed that it mentioned an off date but that the Yankees are going to have a workout. So I thought, "Oh, that'll be a good day to go because there won't be as many kids around. Maybe I can get the fellows that I didn't get yet to sign the ball." So I got down there early, and there weren't many kids. The first man to come along was Frank Crosetti. I recognized him right away. And I said, "Mr. Crosetti, could you sign the ball?" And he said, "Sure."

Then I realized I was lacking two signatures to have the whole team, including the managers and the coaches. One of the major people was the Yankee manager, a very renowned man, Joe McCarthy. I thought, "I really should go home. But I'll wait a little longer." Now it was down to two kids. I waited, and sure enough he comes out. And I asked him, "Mr. Mc-Carthy, will you sign the ball? I just need your signature and one other." He didn't say much, he signed the ball. And if you see the ball, it's pretty strong handwriting. So now I'm down to one, who was a reserve catcher. I waited and waited. And now I'm the only one there. Well, sure enough he comes out, and I ran up to him. His name was Rollie Hemsley, and I said, "Mr. Hemsley, will you sign my ball?" He said, "Get out of here, kid!" I said, "Oh, come on. You're the only one. If you sign it, I'll have everybody on the team." He said, "Get out of here, kid!" I just followed him, and I kept asking him. And finally he says, "All right, give me the ball." And he signed it and that was that.

And sure enough it was the '43 Yankees—the world championship team.

January 18, 2004

REBECCA KATECHIS, 51, speaks with her sister CAROLYN SCHLAM, 59

RECORDED IN MIAMI, FLORIDA

Rebecca Katechis: We come from very humble beginnings. We grew up in a very crowded apartment. Everybody was working. We weren't wealthy.

Carolyn Schlam: When our family came from Europe, they were poor. There were six children, three boys and three girls. And they moved into a one-bedroom apartment in the Bronx. The grandfather and the three boys lived in the living room, and Grandma and the three girls slept in the bedroom. They had in this apartment one comfortable chair. That's it—just one comfortable chair. And they would fight over this chair. So these were our humble beginnings. We came from people who fought over a chair. We lived in a very chaotic environment, and the apartment seemed very small.

Rebecca: One of the reasons it seemed so small was that there were always so many people in it. Grandma lived with us. Mommy and Daddy had the other bedroom. And the three of us girls were all stuck together in another bedroom. And that would have been crowded enough, but every night one of the aunts or uncles were over for dinner or over for coffee or playing mah-jongg or just dropping by, and the house was constantly full of people.

Carolyn: In some houses maybe there's music playing in the background. I don't remember any music ever playing in the background because the music of our lives was the voices. The conversation, the constant conversation. And most of those voices were female voices.

Rebecca: Those female voices were in the kitchen cooking elaborate meals. Even if it was just a regular school night, they were cooking meals that would have several courses. And during the dinner everybody would be talking at once and talking very fast.

Carolyn: It was almost like a contest. It was just something that you were expected to be good at. Even though the quality of their language was so rich, the actual subject matter was the most inane, insignificant stuff. Mommy would go to the supermarket, and she'd come back and she'd do forty-five minutes on the bargains at Olinsky's. Even though they were common people, the thing that is most amazing about them was that they had personality plus! That's what they had, and that's what they transmitted to us. But when we were kids, we hated this.

Rebecca: I think we would have killed for a moment of privacy. And I think we must have said to each other a thousand times, "When are these people leaving? Oh my God, Uncle Mack is here! Oh my God, Uncle Sol!" And as children in those years you had to cleave to a certain amount of politeness, and so you had to go out and get a big wet kiss from Uncle Mack. We rebelled against it, and I think there was a long period of time that we didn't appreciate it.

Carolyn: We've come a long way. And now at this point in our lives, we're at the same age as our parents were during the period that we're describing, and I see them in a completely different light. I only see the positives. I only see the joy.

They were able to turn the ordinary into something absolutely splendid. And I think in the end if we asked them, "Did you have a successful life?" all of them would have said, "Yes." They loved. They had friends. They were alive. They didn't see the world, but they saw their world—which maybe is better than seeing the world.

If Mommy and Aunt Lee and our sister Toby came into this room right now, what would you like to say to them?

Rebecca: I would say, "Yes, I hated how you were, but I like it now. I would like to be a fifty-year-old woman like you! I really think you did a good job."

Carolyn: What I'd like to say is "I was a bad daughter." Oh, boy, did I give my mother trouble with all of my rebelliousness! "But, Mommy, I thank you. I know I was wrong. I was young. I am so sorry that we never got to have a rapprochement. I'm so sorry I couldn't be like a friend to you, and you couldn't know me as the adult that I've become. And we promise that we will carry on as best as we can the wonderful traditions that you have handed down to us."

Rebecca: The stuff of life was meager. There was one chair. The apartment was stuffy. Who wanted to talk about Olinsky's when the Vietnam War was raging and we wanted to go out there and change it? And how dare you scratch my Bob Dylan record! But in the end we want to say to them,

"Thanks for teaching us to talk. Thanks for teaching us to be of the world and in the world and to make our way. Thanks for teaching us to be alive! And thanks for staying inside of us."

February 13, 2006

*Rebecca Katechis (l.) and
Carolyn Schlam (r.)*

WORK

and

DEDICATION

Facilitators are both the core and *corps* of StoryCorps—the project's frontline workers and ambassadors who accompany participants through the interview process. The qualifications are simple: They must be extraordinary listeners and have a quality about them that puts people at ease.

Facilitators are hired for a one-year term and typically spend nine months working in New York City and three months on the road with one of our mobile booths. Any number of facilitators have told me that the most important lesson they learn over the course of their service has to do with judging others: Never assume from how people look that you understand who they really are. Many also say they've come to recognize a simple truth: that people are basically good.

At the end of the facilitators' one-year terms of service, they're sprinkled back out into the world, having recorded hundreds of stories and listened in on the wisdom of humanity.

DR. MONICA MAYER, 45,
interviewed by her cousin and patient,
SPENCER WILKINSON JR., 39

RECORDED IN NEW TOWN, NORTH DAKOTA

Spencer Wilkinson Jr.: What made you choose to pursue a career in medicine?

Dr. Monica Mayer: My father was full-blood German, and my mother was full-blood Indian, and it was pretty tough in the sixties growing up half-breed, so to speak. My father didn't have any sons, so he raised us like little boys. And I must have been in about seventh grade, and I wasn't doing well in school. In fact, I was maybe getting Cs, and I'm the oldest of three girls. So my dad packed us up in his pickup truck and took us out to his old homestead land, which is about eighteen miles north of New Town, in the middle of nowhere. Well, New Town's kind of in the middle of nowhere, but, I mean, this is *really* in the middle of nowhere. And he packed us some lunches and some water. He dropped us off out there at seven or eight in the morning and said he wanted all the rocks picked up and put in the northwest corner in one big pile and that he'd come back that night to pick us up, and it had better be done.

So there we were, working hard all day, and then he comes back. And we're dirty, stinky, sweaty, sore muscles, crying. My dad pulls up, and he gets out of the pickup. And we must have been a sight to see. I looked at him and I said, since I was the oldest—my two younger sisters are hiding behind me—"Dad, we don't think this is fair we have to work this hard." And I remember him saying, "Is that right? Well, do you think I like working hard like this every day?" "No." He said, "You know, your mother said you girls don't like school and you're not doing very well. So I talked to Momma, and we decided that you're going to come out here and work like this so your hind ends will get used to how your life's going to be when you get older." So I said, "Well, if we got good grades, do we have to come out here and work this hard?" And he said, "No. That's the deal."

Well, he didn't have to bust my head twice up against the brick wall. My two younger sisters and I were laughing about that, because they remember that particular day exactly the way I remembered it. One day of hard labor changed everything.

July 29, 2005

Today, Monica Mayer practices family medicine on the Fort Berthold reservation in New Town, North Dakota. Her sister Holly is the Director of Public Health Nurses on the reservation, and her sister Renee is Tribal Social Services Director.

KEN KOBUS, 58, tells his friend
RON BARAFF, 42, about making steel

RECORDED IN PITTSBURGH, PENNSYLVANIA

Ken Kobus: Both of my grandfathers worked in the mill. My father started in 1937. I started about twenty-nine years later, in 1966, at the same plant. I was always enthralled with steel from the time I was a very young person. I always wanted to go into the mill, but I was always too young to go. And finally when I turned sixteen, I told my dad that he had to take me— and I bugged him until he did.

You look at it from his point of view, he was a union guy. And for him to come to the mill on his day off, he had to take a bit of harassment for it: "What the heck are you doing here?" My dad had straight dark black hair; his nickname was Crow. When we finally got into the mill, they said, "Crow, what are you doing here? It's your day off! Are you crazy?" At the same time, though, he was very proud. He thought enough to bring his son into the place that he worked.

When I went into the shop, I was actually a little bit frightened. All these things were moving back and forth, and I was afraid I was going to get run over and didn't know where to move. My dad just walked straight through like nothing was going on. Steelmaking is just beautiful. It's unimaginable beauty. When you're charging a furnace, you get all these sparkles off of the iron, and so you just see thousands and thousands of sparkles.

We proceeded into the plant, and my dad went over and talked to the boss of the shop. I found out that they were going to tap a furnace. I remember it like yesterday, although it's now forty-two years later. We went over to the furnace, and I found out that they were going to let me tap the furnace. When we went over, a lot of the guys started gathering around. Even though I was sixteen, I recognized that something was strange. This probably is not the way it is normally done. But I didn't really care because I was going to get to tap the furnace, and if these guys want to watch, fine with me.

There was a battery box with a switch and a little button that you used to set off the dynamite charge and the foreman said, "When I tell you to, flip the switch; and when I tell you to tap, press the button." And my dad came to me and says, "I don't care what you do," he says, "don't let go of that battery box."

So came time and they blew the siren for "all clear" and then waited a little bit just to make sure that nobody's below, because when this steel lets loose, sparks go everywhere. It came time to flip the switch, and then it came time to press the button. The dynamite blew up and made such a god-awful sound, and there was smoke and fire and sparks everywhere. And then the steel started running into the spout, and there were flames shooting up out of the spout, and I jumped up in the air. I must have jumped three, four feet in the air, I was so scared. And then I knew why all these guys were around. They started laughing, because it was such a sight to see somebody so scared. I was the show for that day, and they had their good laugh on me.

But it was spectacular. The steel starting running and went into the ladle. When it hits the bottom of the ladle, it goes *splunch* and makes all kinds of different sounds that you never expect. What do you think happens when 2,900-degree steel hits finely powdered coal that's lying in the bottom of the ladle? Well, it creates a fire that you just can't imagine. The fire almost hit the roof of the shop, and it was eighty feet above you, and you're standing right beside this ladle of running steel. And the supervisor is not telling the guys to run away; he's telling them, "Throw some bags here" and "Throw some this there." There's all these people moving around, and there's all this heat, and it's just an unforgettable experience.

Two years later I started working in the mills. I worked in the foundry. I was the third helper on the electric furnace, and I worked various jobs in the steel foundry.

Ron Baraff: If you could choose any job in the steel mill, what would it be?

Ken: Oh, I'd choose my dad's job. He was a first helper, in charge of an open-hearth furnace. To face a furnace is just— It's hard to describe because when you open a door of the furnace, it's at over 3,000 degrees, and your whole body's standing in front of a door opened to hell. It has effects on your body; it stretches your skin. And you watch cold steel, scrap metal, being put into there, and you just watch it become more and more red and red and red, and then it just sort of like disappears and falls apart. You see huge, huge boiling steel—it's not water, it's steel. And you see these bubbles and these balls flopping out and it's just like a volcano. You're looking in a volcano.

I know it stuck with my father for all his life. I mean, when he was dying, he couldn't talk. He had throat cancer, and so they took his voice box out—and he was in a lot of pain. I was in the hospice, and I was watching him in the bed once and the doctor came in. He saw that I was looking at my dad, and my dad was lying on his back and he had his hands up in the air, and he was turning and manipulating. The doctor says, "I wonder what the heck he's doing." Because, you know, he did it all the time. He would be lying on his back, and he would be doing this stuff, and they had no clue as to what he was doing. I said, "He's making steel." I could see what he was doing. He was opening furnace doors, and he was adjusting the gas on the furnace and the draft. I could see. The doctor was amazed. To the day he died that's what he lived: steelmaking. And that's quite an impression. And it's made an impression on me, too. I could always recommend to somebody to watch steel being born. It's just fantastic. It's a spectacle that is unreal.

I've been working for forty years, and it's just long, hard work. A lot of times I can't imagine how the men bear up against it. The guys knew how to work and could face up to the job and just were so strong. I was proud to be around many guys that could do that, that wanted to do that, and had pride in doing that. They took pride in what they did. And they knew that people looked at them with honor. They made steel.

June 20, 2006

Ken Kobus (l.) and Ron Baraff (r.)

SAMUEL W. BLACK, 45, interviewed by his wife, EDDA FIELDS-BLACK, 34

RECORDED IN PITTSBURGH, PENNSYLVANIA

Edda Fields-Black: The reason I asked you here today was because your father passed away on June 18, 2004. I wanted to make this CD to tell our son some things about his grandfather.

Samuel W. Black: My father started working for the Cincinnati public schools around 1955, and he worked primarily as a janitor. Daddy would come home tired to the bone. And he worked late hours, especially in the wintertimes because you had to keep the school warm twenty-four hours a day to keep the pipes from freezing. What I remember as a little boy is he would come home and just fall out on the bed. And I remember he would sleep with his arms up like that, and we'd climb on him and squeeze his muscles. There were times when he would ask us to rub his feet, and we hated it. I mean, he'd be working sixteen-hour days, and you'd have to take his socks off and rub the feet. You hated to walk past his bedroom 'cause he'd call you in there and ask you to do that. But looking back on it, his body was probably killing him, and he was being soothed by his little boys.

In 1977, when I was in high school, he took me down to the boiler room in that bad winter in Cincinnati when it was 20 degrees below zero. By the time I was there, the building was sixty-seven years old, took up a huge city block, five stories. So we're down in the boiler room and it's 20 below zero outside, and we're down there with no shirt on. It's probably over 100 degrees down there. You have these huge boilers, and they have these steel doors that you open up and you can see the coal burning in there. And you just got to keep the fire going. And so you have these shovels that are maybe fifteen feet long, and you stick the shovel in there and you turn the coals over. Then you close the door and push a set of buttons, and you can hear the coal falling down in those huge pipes into the fire. I remember it was so hot. The boiler room was so loud it was like you were on an ocean liner. If the phone rang, the lights would blink on and off, that's how you knew the phone was ringing. It was just such a loud, steaming hot, dirty coal place. You blow your nose, and all this coal dust would just come out of your nose.

That's when I knew: I'm not doing this for a living. I said, "No, not me."

June 9, 2006

66

JOYCE BUTLER, 73, interviewed by her daughter STEPHANIE BUTLER, 47

RECORDED IN PORTLAND, MAINE

Joyce Butler: My parents divorced in 1941. In those days divorce was not as common as it is now. A divorced woman was called a "grass widow," and grass widows were scorned. There was a stigma attached, which is why it took such courage for my mother to ask for a divorce from my father. We moved to Maine Avenue in Portland.

Even though my father paid my mother money every month, it wasn't enough. She had to go to work, and she had not finished high school. So she worked in the laundry, and she finally got a job at Montgomery Ward department store on Congress Street. And we kids were more or less on our own. That was not a happy time for me—I missed my mother.

During the war, the shipyard had begun to function in South Portland, and these young women would come into the store, all dressed in these big boots and rough overalls. And they would have checks of six hundred dollars to cash for their shopping. She finally asked, "Where do you work that you make so much money?" They said, "In the shipyard." So my mother went over and tried to get a job. The man who interviewed asked if she wanted to be a welder or a burner, and my mother said, "Which pays the most?" And he said, "A welder." And she said, "That's what I want to do." And he said, "Oh, a mercenary, huh?" And she said, "No. I have four children to take care of."

Her shift was midnight to 6:00 A.M., so she could be home with us during the day. I remember her dressing in that heavy clothing and big boots—men's clothing. Once she fell and hurt her ankle, and they brought her home in the middle of the night, and she was weeping. It was awful.

It was bitter cold in the winter, going into the bowels of those steel ships. They had to wiggle into narrow crawl spaces and lay on their backs and weld overhead. She was very thin in those years, but I remember her neck and her chest, all spotted with burn marks from the sparks. They had to wear special goggles, but even so, sometimes they would have a flash condition in their eyes. She suffered from that, and they had to take her to the hospital once.

After the shipyard closed, she went back to Montgomery Ward and worked all day. And at five o'clock when she got out of Montgomery Ward, she got on a bus and worked in the S. D. Warren Paper Mill from six o'clock until midnight. Came home, got up in the morning, and went back to Montgomery Ward.

Stephanie Butler: Bless her heart.

Joyce: My mother wanted to keep us together as a family. She was determined.

September 7, 2006

Work and Dedication

SHARON ST. AUBIN, 57, interviewed by her nephew JERROLD ARNESON, 33

RECORDED IN BISMARCK, NORTH DAKOTA

Sharon St. Aubin: Blaisdell, North Dakota, was a very small town. I'm afraid someday it won't even be on the map anymore. Only about sixty-five people lived in Blaisdell at the time I was growing up. Your mother and I got to know everybody in town, because your grandmother ran the post office.

The front room of our house was the post office, and it was open many hours so that people could come in and pick up their mail. And people did come in at all hours. A lot of people didn't lock their doors, but we always did, because my mom said, "We have that federal mail in here, so we have to lock it."

Every morning, except Sunday, Mom opened up the post office and put up the flag. Mom was very careful that the flag never touched the ground and that we got it in before it was dark. And right by the flagpole there was a flower bed. Some mornings somebody would have fallen into her flower bed because the bar was right next door to us, and she'd be really upset because some of her favorite flowers would get broken off.

She had to meet the train, because the train was how the mail went out. She would sort the mail and put it in a bag with a lock on it. We'd go down to the depot, and we'd crawl up a little ladder, and we would hang the mailbag from an arm that came out. And when the train came by, they had a long device that would grab the bag. We had to stay there till that train left, because if they went to grab that bag and the bag went flying, we had to go pick it up.

I remember sitting in that train depot. It was not air-conditioned like this room is today, and Grandma—your grandma, my mother—would have poetry books. And she would memorize poetry. And we would sit with the book, and she would say the poem. And we'd prompt her if she'd forget. Sometimes the train came very late, so we'd sit for hours, just listening to Mom do this poetry.

Every spring the farmers that raised chickens got baby chicks that came by mail. Your mom and I loved that, because the baby chicks came in high cardboard boxes that had air holes on the sides, and those little baby chicks would be chirping in there. When the people came to pick them up, Grandma would open up the lid, and she would count the baby chicks and see if there were any dead ones and record it, because the people were insured and would be reimbursed for the dead ones. One spring there was a blizzard, and we had the baby chicks, and people couldn't get there to pick them up. And, of course, we didn't have any chicken feed. But Mom had oatmeal. So she brought them into the kitchen, and we got to sprinkle oatmeal in there, and we put little dishes of water in there, and I thought it was great.

My mom didn't want the post office to look bad in any way, so we took care of the chicks.

July 20, 2005

LORI FITZGERALD, 36, interviews
her father, LENDALL HILL, 58

RECORDED IN CHARLESTON, WEST VIRGINIA

Lori Fitzgerald: You grew up near Rock, West Virginia, a very small, very rural area. What was it like?

Lendall Hill: We resided in hardscrabble farmland. The school bus stop was at Dad's sawmill, so as soon as I got off the bus in the evening, I went down to the sawmill. While Dad was sharpening the circle saws and so forth, I would load the truck, usually by myself, so Dad could get up at three in the morning to deliver to the mines.

As you know, my dad got his leg cut off in a farming accident just before I was born. At that time the artificial legs were made out of paper with varnish; they were put around a mold, and there were cables in the ankles that connected the leg to the foot. He was learning to walk again about the same time I was learning to walk. So I grew up with my dad's artificial leg, and things would happen.

One time we were delivering mining materials, and there was a timber checker that had to look at every header [support beam] that we were unloading. And these headers weighed anywhere between 200 and 240 pounds apiece. Dad had to pick every one of those up on the truck and turn it over so the man could see all four edges of it. And Dad pulled one of the headers out and got his artificial leg caught, and as he turned, he snapped one of the cables. It let out a pretty loud pop, and he said, "Oh, darn, I think I broke my foot!" He came walking across the truck, and the foot was turned at right angles to what it should be. And he caught that foot in his two hands, and he straightened it up. It cracked and popped something awful. And that timber checker turned white as cotton. We didn't think anything about it.

Several years later Uncle Lon, Dad's brother, had run into the guy. He asked him, he said, "Lon, are you any kin to Vaughn Hill that used to deliver mining materials?" Lon said, "Sure, that's my brother." The timber checker said, "I'll tell you one thing," he said. "That's the toughest man I've ever seen." He said, "When he broke his foot, he just set that thing and finished unloading that truck." Well, Uncle Lon was laughing so hard, he said tears were rolling down his cheeks. He never told the guy that it was an artificial leg that Dad was working with.

Another episode: Mr. Lineback was a gentleman over in Bluewell, West Virginia, who was about the only one in a three-state area that could fix circle saws when one got damaged. One day we went to Mr. Lineback's, and by the time we got over there, he had already closed his shop. There was a gate, and on this gate was a sign that said Beware Vicious Dog. He had this large German shepherd. Dad started walking in, and I said, "Dad, you really want to go over there? You know that dog's a mean one." He said, "I got to get this saw fixed." He looks around and doesn't see the dog anywhere, so he walks through the gate. I stop and close the gate, me on the safe side.

He gets about two steps, and here comes that dog around the house, not growling or anything, just white fangs. And that dog grabs Dad's artificial leg, and he lets out a huge howl, and he goes running back around behind the house. He looks out around the corner of the house, he barks, and he jerks his head back. And he looks out around the corner of the house and barks again. Well, Dad went right on over to conduct his business with Mr. Lineback.

Anyway, a week later we go back to pick up the saw. Mr. Lineback said, "Mr. Hill, did you do something to that dog of mine?" Dad says, "No, I didn't do anything to him. When I came in, he grabbed me by the leg and bit it." "Well, I'll tell you one thing," Mr. Lineback says. "He's worthless now. When somebody comes by, he runs around behind the house and hides."

Dad never did get around to telling him: When he went to take off his pants that night, he had two prime canine teeth buried in that artificial leg, pinning his pants to his leg.

There were some interesting times with that old leg.

June 24, 2005

BARB FULLER-CURRY, 68, interviewed by her son, CRAIG CURRY, 34

RECORDED IN CHICAGO, ILLINOIS

Craig Curry: When I come and visit you out in the country, every once in a while a combine or a tractor will drive by in front of the house. A lot of times you'll cry when you see them. Why is that?

Barb Fuller-Curry: I cry because I'm so proud of how hard my mom and dad worked. When I was a young child, I didn't appreciate it, but now I do. It's a wonderful legacy. We still have the family farm, and I'm tremendously proud of that.

I think I was in almost my forties or fifties before I realized the sacrifices they made. They were married during the Depression. When I was younger, in the wintertime my dad would get up around four in the morning to start chores. In the winter they had to light little kerosene heaters for the water for the livestock. He'd have to go out all bundled up, dealing with water at 10 below zero. He would start his chores around four in the morning—and then around seven, he would come in for breakfast. He'd have breakfast with me—as a family we would—before I went off to school. I just remembered the coziness of that kitchen, sitting at a big walnut table. And I can always remember my mother saying that there was always room at the table for one more. No matter who came, we'd always make room.

I can remember one time in particular. I had to be maybe

six or seven years old, and it had been a very wet spring. They were all just small family farms, probably 100 to 150 acres. But it would take a long time to harvest or plant even that much with the equipment that they had. My dad was getting behind with planting the corn and soybeans, so he rigged up lights on the tractor. I can still see it: He mounted lights on the front of the tractor so that they could farm at night. Daddy would work in the field all day, then come in for supper. After we would have our evening meal, Mom would go out to the field, and Mom was farming at night.

I can remember, after I'd had my bath upstairs, we would go to the window and listen to see if the tractor was still running and Mom was okay. I can still remember those nights. I can still remember sitting there, listening for my mom out in the field. I often think how they had to be so wise and ingenious to rig all this up and get the corn planted in time. I lost my mom in May, and I appreciate so much everything she did for me. Mom was—as my dad always said—the best hired man he ever had.

August 28, 2005

**RICK KINCAID, 53, interviewed
by his friend DANNY TERRY, 60**

RECORDED IN AUSTIN, TEXAS

Rick Kincaid: I was born in Tyler, Texas, and grew up in Cayuga, Texas. We used to make the comment that we were so far back in the woods, we had to go towards town to hunt. We came from basically uneducated families and backwoods hillbilly folks. Nobody had any money. We were just dirt poor.

My mother was a Pentecostal preacher, so there was always a battle between her and my dad as far as living a good life. She wanted him off the road from playing what we used to call "hillbilly music" and wanted him in the church playing gospel music. He finally did give it up, and him and Mother got a tent and we had a tent revival in the '50s. We traveled all around east Texas and put that tent up preachin' revivals. There was a lot of unusual things for a little boy my age to be seeing in those days. They would cast out demons in them tents, and then that night we had to sleep in there—so it was a little scary. We figured the devil's gonna hang around and get ahold of us, so I'd sleep there in that old cot and put Bibles all around me.

Probably the thing that scared me the most about the religion I was raised up in—Mother being, like I said, a Pentecostal preacher—she was also what they call a "prophet." I remember one night my mother stopped a service right in the middle of her preaching, and she approached a man sitting on a bench and told him that she saw the number 3 over his head, and that meant if he didn't get saved that night and give his heart to the Lord, he was going to be dead in three days. It wasn't what she said that night that scared me, but three days later that man fell dead in his kitchen. Was an aneurysm in his brain. That scared me.

I was twenty-five years old when Occidental Petroleum hired me. I ended up as a welder in the oil field until the oil field failed. In 1980 there were no jobs in the petroleum industry. I had a friend was a bail bondsman, and I worked for him. One day we hired a feller to chase one down for us, and seeing how much money he was making, I figured I wanted to do that. So I spent eleven years as a bounty hunter.

When a man goes to jail for a certain crime, the judge will set this man's bond, and the bail bondsman will bail this man out for a certain fee. Now this man is obligated to show up to court on a certain day. If the feller doesn't show up, they assume that he has absconded. A lot of times a bail bondsman will try to find him. If they're unsuccessful, then they'll call in a bounty hunter. Our job is to go find this man and get him arrested. There's probably three or four hundred people that I've chased down and locked up. I worked in Texas, New Mexico, Oklahoma, Louisiana, Florida. We built up a good reputation as real hard-nosed bounty hunters. We got a reputation to where some fellers would find out we were chasing them, and they'd just put their self in jail.

There was one young feller where it became a matter of principle. He really wasn't in all that much trouble. I think I was only getting about three hundred dollars to pick him up.

But every time we'd go to his house, he would take off out that back door and hit them woods, and we just couldn't catch him. So after three or four times going to this young man's house to pick him up and he always ran on us, we decided one night we were going to get him. We went over by my uncle's house and picked up an old fishin' net, and we strapped that thing around the front porch of his house. We beat on the back door, and he took off out the front and got tangled up in that net. We got him in jail by three o'clock that morning. It became a pretty good joke around Smith County on how he got caught.

Probably one of the toughest cases we had—I won't call the old boy's name out, but he was from Sulphur Springs, Texas, and there was a one-hundred-thousand-dollar jump bond on him. When we started chasing him, it was for aggravated kidnapping on his ex-wife. However, once we got the job and signed the contract, we come to find out that he was a big-time methamphetamine drug dealer. So we figured we were up against a little bit more than we had originally bargained for. I chased him for about seven months. That was a long, hard chase. We had several problems catching this old boy.

The night that we got him, some of the Cherokee County Sheriff Department was supposed to hit the house about the same time I did. I went in first, and unbeknownst to them or us, it was a drug lab. I walked right in the middle of it, and they got me on the floor and began to beat me pretty good. They broke my jaw and my cheekbone and knocked out a couple of my teeth. Then they started asking questions and began to pull my teeth out with some old pliers. 'Course I really couldn't answer any questions—I was in too much pain. So I was sure proud to see when the sheriff department finally did break in there and get me out of that. I figured that was going to be the end.

And that was the night I retired from bounty hunting. I walked down the road to where my wife was sitting in the van and told her that I would be retiring that night. That was about as close to death as I wanted to get.

April 30, 2006

*Danny Terry (l.) and
Rick Kincaid (r.)*

Retired police detective PHYLLIS
JOHNSON, 54, interviewed by her friend
DANNY PERASA, 65

RECORDED IN NEW YORK CITY

Danny Perasa: How did you come to get on the police
force?

Phyllis Johnson: I was working in the precinct as a clerk.
My job was to take the reports from police officers and type
them up on the forms. And I used to fuss and say, "These guys,
they don't know how to write! Their grammar's atrocious!"
And one of the cops said, "You think you can do better?" And
I said, "Yes, I can." So he takes an application for the police
department, and he throws it at me. He says, "Here. Fill this
out. I'll even pay your filing fee." And so I filled it out, and
the next thing I know, they call me to join the police force.

After the first day of being sworn in, they gave us these big
black bags filled with books. It was so heavy, and I remember
struggling on the subway. I got off and I'm walking down the
street, and a police car rolled up and said, "Hey, kid. You think
you can do that?" Because I was so small—I was only like
ninety-eight pounds at the time. And that just made me more
determined than ever, because I said, "Who does this guy think
I am? I can do it just as well as he can!"

My first assignment, they sent me out to Rockaway, Queens.
There was a wife abuser, and he beat her up and threw her out
the window—I think it was the tenth or eleventh floor. And

when we got there, there was this poor woman laying on the ground, and I remember cradling her head in my arms, and I knew she was going to die, and I said, "Honey, don't worry. We got the ambulance coming. Just hang in there." And I said, "What happened? Did you fall? What happened?" She said, "No. My husband pushed me." And I said, "Now, I want you to know you may be dying. Are you telling the truth?" And she said, "I know I'm dying." She says, "Yes. He used to beat me all the time." And so we got her into the hospital, and she did expire in the hospital, and the neighbors told us where we could find him, and we did. We found this guy. He was cowering over somewhere near the boardwalk. And that was my first arrest.

I was in narcotics for a good while. I tried to look as terrible as possible. In fact, when I came out of the locker room and I was all geared up and ready to go out in the street, one of my partners looked at me and says, "You look like a disease." There were many times when I would go into court because we made these arrests of these drug dealers, and they said, "Okay. Now we're going to bring the undercover in," and when I walked in and sat down on the stand you'd see the reaction of this person who had sold drugs to me, and they actually slink down in the chair, because it's like "Oh my God—her?" They'd never thought it could've been me that was actually the one responsible for them being locked up.

Danny: How soon after 9/11 did you leave the department?

Phyllis: It was three months to the day, December 11. We were assigned to go to the Staten Island dump, because that's where they were taking all the debris. They told us, "You have several buckets here." There was a bucket for body parts. And there was a bucket if you found anything that would identify a person—whether it be a wallet or jewelry or anything like that. So I did that until the day before Veteran's Day. I was at the dump that night, and it was pouring down raining, and I remember I had my Hazmat suit on, and I was so tired. And I just turned a bucket over, and I sat down on this bucket in the dump. And the methane gas was starting to bubble up through all of this dirt, and all the water was just pouring down in my face, and I said, "God, I can't do this anymore. I just can't do it anymore."

The very next day I went down to One Police Plaza and I told them, "I want to put in my papers," and they said, "But there's nobody here to tell you how much money you're going to end up with." I said, "I don't care. Just get my papers in order." I turned in my weapons, and when I walked out of the front door of One Police Plaza, I never looked back.

July 19, 2004

. . . .

Bus driver RONALD RUIZ, 57, interviewed by facilitator BRETT MYERS, 27

RECORDED IN NEW YORK CITY

Ronald Ruiz: I love my passengers. I remember one woman in particular—a senior who had gotten on my bus. She seemed completely lost. She said she was going to a restaurant on City Island Avenue. I could see she was confused. There was just something about her. She looked so elegant, but with a fur coat on a hot summer day, so I said, "Are you okay?" She said, "I'm fine, but I don't know what restaurant I'm meeting my friends at." I said, "Get on. Sit in the front." I asked a gentleman to get up so she could sit near me, and I said, "I'll run in, and I'll check each restaurant for you."

So I checked the restaurants, and no luck, but at the very, very last restaurant on the left, I said, "It's got to be this one. Let me swing the bus around," and I swung it around. I said, "Don't move. Let me make sure this is the place before you get out." It was a hot day, and she's got a fur on. She could pass out. So I said, "Stay here, sweetie. It's nice and cool in here." I went in and I said, "There's a lady in the bus, and she's not sure of the restaurant," and I saw a whole bunch of seniors there, and they said, "Oh, that's her!"

I ran back to the bus and I said, "Sweetie, your restaurant is right here." I said, "Let me kneel the bus." Kneeling the bus means I bring it closer to the ground so she gets off easier. And I said, "Don't move." I remember my right hand grabbed her right hand. I wanted to make her feel special, like it was a limousine. It was a bus, but I wanted to make her feel like it was a limousine. And she said, "I've been diagnosed with cancer—but today is the best day of my life."

And I never forgot that woman. (*Weeping.*) She's diagnosed with cancer, and just because I helped her off the bus, she said she felt like Cinderella. Can't get better than that. And doing your job and getting paid to do a job where you can do something special like that? It's pretty awesome.

July 28, 2004

. . . .

BARNEY FELDMAN, 87, interviewed by his daughter, SUSAN BECKMAN, 65

RECORDED IN SAN DIEGO, CALIFORNIA

Barney Feldman: My father came from Russia, and he was a barber. He had a barbershop, and every time a new baby was born, he added a barber chair to pay for the baby that came. That was in Cincinnati, Ohio. At my particular time there were eight children and eight chairs. Each chair had a barber. When I was little enough to walk, my mother would tell my dad, "Take Barney to the barbershop," which meant it would be one less child at home for her to take care of.

I would sit all day with the head porter, John. A porter in those days in a barbershop gave free shines and furnished their own polish. They swept the hair off the floor and washed the windows and kept things clean in exchange for being there to give free shines. It was really a coup to get into a barbershop to give shines. This was during the Depression.

I was told when I was ten years old, "Barney, when you're big enough to be a porter, I'll show you how to make tips. The first thing you do is brush the hair off their shoulders. Then you help them on with their coat. Before you help them on with their coat, you brush their pants pockets. If you don't hear any change with the brushing of their pockets, they won't give you a tip."

I finally got to the point where I was a doorman, and the barbers would say, "Barney, get me a customer." I'd rattle the old-fashioned door handle to attract someone from the street, and he'd come over—always a man that needed a haircut. He'd come over and say, "What do you want?" And I'd say, "You need a haircut." I'd catch a customer once in a while because in those days haircuts were only twenty-five cents and singes were free.

Susan Beckman: What's a singe?

Barney: A free singe in those days was to lightly burn the freshly cut hair, to seal the hair so it won't fall apart. So that was free. But the smell was as if you had burnt the feathers off of a chicken, so that would mean you needed a shampoo, which was seventy-five cents.

When I got older, we had this man, Old Man Pete, who lived across the street. He had a defect in his spine and never could stand up straight. He was always bent over as if he was picking up a quarter off the sidewalk. He always did odd jobs. After I got married, there was a truck that would deliver coal. It would back up into the driveway, and we had a window that went to the cellar. It would take me two or three days to shovel five tons of coal into the cellar. One day I asked Old Man Pete would he want to shovel in five tons of coal? He said, "Sure, I'll do it." So the next load that came—it was wintertime—I went across the street to where he lived, and I said, "How much would you want?" He said, "A dollar a ton." He made five dollars.

About thirty minutes later the doorbell rings, and Old Man Pete's at the door. I said, "You all done?" He said, "Oh, yeah, I'm done. You got the five dollars?" I gave him the five dollars, and I said, "How did you get that coal in there so quickly?" He said, "I'll tell you how it's done. You take the shovel, you fill it up with coal in one big scoop, and then you put it in the window. Keep doing it in a motion that's constant and don't look up to see what you have left. The trick is to not look up to how much more you have to do but to just keep doing it. If your body goes into a motion of shoveling and tossing it, shoveling and tossing it in, all the sudden you have no more to shovel." That's where I learned when you have a job to do, don't keep looking up to see how much left there is to do. If you keep working at your job, it'll be done. That was one piece of advice that I've lived by.

I've had forty-five different jobs in my lifetime. Most of them I was never qualified for. I'm an artist, a sculptor, a plumber. I would say I have a doctorate degree in janitoring. That's the story of Barney Feldman.

February 20, 2006

SCOTT KOHANEK, 52, and his wife, CATHERINE KOHANEK, 51

RECORDED IN NEW YORK CITY

Scott Kohanek: We've talked a lot over the years about how we met each other. I think back to those first weeks at Kenwood Elementary in Minneapolis, where I was a custodian and you were a special ed teacher. My first question to you is: Do you recall the first moment that you said to yourself, "I'm going to marry that guy"?

Catherine Kohanek: No. But I do remember watching you move around the school. You were sliding down the banisters, and you were popping bubble gum. That's one of the first impressions I had of you: "Who is this guy who lives in the world of kids?"

Scott: And acts like one.

Catherine: And acts like one. And then I watched you with your guitar, getting in the classrooms and singing, and getting so involved with the kids. And I said to myself, "Why is this guy a custodian?" I mean, we need custodians, and thank God there's custodians, but you seemed destined for something else. But there you were—you were thirty-three or thirty-four—and so I think I asked you, "Why aren't you a teacher?" And then I found out that you graduated from high school when you were seventeen, which was half your life ago, and maybe you didn't think college was meant for you or you couldn't cut it.

You would talk to me when you came in my classroom and emptied my trash. You would always sit on the counter by the door, and you would start to ask me questions. I remember a particular conversation where one of the questions you asked was "Are you happy?" You know, a lot of people ask, "How are you feeling today?" But no—you looked right at me and you said, "Are you happy?" I was going through a hard time in my life, and up to that point I had kind of been pretending with friends and family that I was happy. But I wasn't happy. I kind of wondered what you saw, because I know you saw something. So that really sticks out in my mind. I remember thinking, "This person is seeing into me." And it scared me actually.

Scott: That was a favorite place of mine to sit, on the counter, with my feet up on the chair. And I was always ready for a conversation with you because every time we got past a certain point of riding the surface-type questions, we got kind of deep kind of fast. And we'd always seem to talk about things that really mattered. It was the best time of my day, because people would often say, "Hey, why are you working so fast? You look like you're in a hurry." Well, I had things to get done, because I knew exactly what I wanted to do at the end of the day—go hang out in your room.

Catherine: What's funny is that's not my recollection. It was almost like it was very casual. I'd just sit there and do my paperwork at the end of the day and watch the clock. I could hear you coming down the hall, because you were pushing the big rolling garbage can, so I could kind of gauge where you were, and I knew what side of the hall you were on. And

I'm looking at the clock going, "Gosh, I wonder if he's going to roll that garbage can around here before three-thirty?" But it always seemed very casual when you showed up. It didn't seem like it was planned or plotted or whatever. And then, boom—there you were in the doorway, and you'd start to ask me questions.

Scott: One of the greatest memories that I have is when we were sitting outside school. It was after my grandfather had died, and I had spent a lot of time with him. I was very close to him, and after he had passed away and was cremated, you asked if I had the remains. And I did. They were in the car. And you said, "Can I see them?" (*Laughter.*) And we took them out. And there was Grandpa inside the box. We had a rather humorous time commenting on what the ashes looked like, and yet showing great respect and recognizing his time on this planet. And that kind of thing brought us together. I kept sensing that here's a person who has enormous insight. I used to often say you talked like I think.

We were, I think, discovering the depth of our relationship and the depth of our care for one another. So that's when I realized that my path was seriously going to change. When I was in my mid-thirties, after eighteen and a half years as a custodian, I stepped into college for the first time. It was constant classes. There were Saturday morning classes and night classes and day classes, and then I'd work the two-to-ten shift.

Catherine: I remember when you first started college. It was after school, and I was in the first-floor hallway. You were pushing your garbage can, and you came up to me really, really excited. You had just started school—maybe you had been in school a month—and you had written your first paper. And I remember you being really nervous about your writing skills and then you got an "A." Do you remember that? You were so happy about that "A," because you didn't have a history of feeling like a successful student.

Scott: It was a big deal to get that first "A." And when I finished school, it came time to get a job. And, lo and behold, it was really strange to find out that there were three openings at Kenwood Elementary. And it just seemed like that was the thing to do. Fate plays a certain hand. And I came back as a second-grade teacher, and that's where I've been ever since.

So there we were, you getting further and further away from the divorce and myself getting four years of college behind me and a new teaching position. And we knew that we were going to spend a life together and that we needed to get married.

Catherine: I remember asking you, "What do you want?"— knowing it would be unconventional. I didn't see a church wedding in our future.

Scott: We did have the conversations about how it wasn't going to be a church; we didn't want to have the ceremony at the courthouse; it wasn't going to be outside. And being a custodian, I knew that schools were used for all kinds of purposes. I remember talking to the head custodian, and he thought it was just a grand idea. So we got married on the stage in the lunchroom and served milk and cookies.

And the tapestry rug that we stood on when we first kissed as husband and wife, that's in my classroom. And I have my chair on it, and I sit there every day, and every day I think about it. I tell my kids the rug is very special so that they don't pick at the fringes. Kids have grabbed it and started pulling on it, and I always tell them, "No, this is the rug I got married on." And they think that it's either very strange or very wonderful, and they leave it alone.

Catherine: It's funny, you know, you and I both work there now. We take our kids down to the lunchroom—"Get in line, kids!"—and every once in a while I just turn my head and I glance up at that stage, and I just smile, you know?

It's hard for me to imagine not being at that school. I can't quite explain it. I imagine working there until I retire. It makes me sad to think about: I have imagined it, packing up my boxes and—jeez, I'm getting teary about a school! *(laughter)*—and walking, driving away from that school for the last time, and not having a room in that school to claim as my own and all those memories of talking to you in the hallways. It would just be strange.

Scott: Kenwood School is part of me. It's part of who I am.

Catherine: There's a feeling about that school, a feeling like home.

April 4, 2006

JANET LUTZ, 62, interviewed by her friend LORI ARMSTRONG, 50

RECORDED IN ATLANTA, GEORGIA

Janet Lutz: I've been a hospital chaplain for most of the last thirty years. I began my work in Chicago and then moved to St. Louis, and I've been at Emory University Hospital for the last sixteen years.

When I was in Chicago, I was working in a hospital that was a level-one trauma center, which is the biggest kind of trauma center there is. And yet it was a very small emergency department. I was the chaplain on call, and there had been a fire, and two little kids were killed from smoke inhalation. The grandmother had tried to rescue them, and her hands had been burned, and they asked me to go and see her. It was such a crowded, busy night that they put her in a storeroom with two other women who were also patients, and they were separated by movable partitions so they couldn't see each other. And I went in to see this woman whose hands had been burned. She was African American, and her two grandchildren had died. She asked me to pray with her, and I started to pray. I would say a sentence, and she would repeat it back to me. And pretty soon the other women that we couldn't see but knew were in this room started to repeat this prayer back also. You know, there's a place in the Bible where Moses is looking at the burning bush, and he takes off his shoes, because it's holy ground. And I really felt in that moment that we ought to take off our shoes, that we were all standing on holy ground, that these three women patients who didn't know each other and couldn't see each other could pray together in this room in the midst of their crisis and pain. Those kinds of moments are the holiest moments I've ever experienced in my life.

When staff are having difficulty, they often call me and ask me to come help them get through their difficulty. There was a group of people in the hospital who weren't getting along, so the department director asked me to interview each one of them individually. They were in the area of the hospital where they packed the surgical instruments before surgery. Each surgery has a list of all the instruments they need, and at the top of the list is the patient's name and then this whole list of instruments. And these technicians work in the basement of the hospital in a huge, cavernous, windowless room with lots of instruments. They're given this list, and it's up to her or to him to pack these instruments in a package and seal them with tape to take up to the O.R. for the particular surgery.

And they were all telling me their stories, and the more I listened to them, the more touched I was by who these people were—people who to most of the hospital were basically anonymous. One of the women told me that as she packed these instruments and she knew the patient's name, she would pray for that patient. And that she had been doing that for forty years. I thought, "No one knows that she's doing this. Nobody knows." Here she is, a person who has been working at that hospital for longer than most of us, who is doing this incredibly important job that has to be done precisely and carefully, and is fairly complicated. And as she's doing this, she's praying for the patients she will never meet and the patients she will never see. She'll never know the outcome. She only knows that she's helping to make their surgery possible.

Then I found out that most of them did it. I interviewed a whole lot of them, and we worked out the issues that they needed to work out in that particular instant, but I think partly what they liked so much was that someone was listening to them, somebody was hearing their story. And that's the key, I think—listening to the stories of the people who are so essential but often not seen by patients and families. They just assume these people are all doing their work, and they don't realize how rich their lives are and how rich their stories are.

One of the things we do each spring that I instituted at the hospital was we go around and bless the hands of all the people who work in the hospital. For me it's a very powerful experience, to touch all of these hands of people. I go around and find the people in the basement, and the people who are cleaning the toilets, and people who are serving the food, and I look for those people to make sure that their hands get blessed. And last year one of them said to me, "This is the most meaningful thing that's ever happened to me, that somebody blessed my hands." That's not something I invented—it's done in a number of hospitals around the country—but it is a very special experience to be able to bless the hands that work, because people work really hard in the hospital. I'm sure they do in other jobs, too, but it's very difficult work, much of what they do. And their hands get dirty. And they're not always as valued as they should be. And so when I go around finding people, wherever they are, to bless their hands, they're often startled and then really touched by it, as am I.

March 11, 2006

JOURNEYS

I n May 2005, StoryCorps launched our two mobile booths from in front of the Library of Congress, and we began airing our stories each Friday morning on NPR. It marked a major turning point. Before then, StoryCorps was little known outside of New York City. Suddenly, we were a national project. The response was astounding. Just weeks after the launch, people were cheering and honking their horns when our Airstream trailer pulled into Missoula, Montana. Reservations for our monthlong visits sold out instantly everywhere we went.

We saw participants driving hundreds of miles to the booths, families arriving hours early in anticipation of their interview. Karen DiMattia, one of our first facilitators on the road, wrote from Portland, Oregon: "People can't get enough of us. This morning I was working in the trailer before we opened and I could hear a man telling his story to the closed door."

Since our launch the mobile booths have crisscrossed the country, stopping everywhere from the nation's largest cities to small towns; from Native American reservations to Fort Bragg, where we collected the stories of soldiers about to leave for Iraq.

Town after town, month after month, our journey continues.

BRITTANY CONANT, 31, interviews her
mother-in-law, MARTHA CONANT, 63

RECORDED IN GREELEY, COLORADO

Martha Conant was aboard United Airlines flight 232, which crashed in Sioux City, Iowa, on July 19, 1989. Of the 296 people on board, 111 perished. Most of the others were seriously injured.

Martha Conant: It was a Wednesday. My recollection is that we left Denver maybe 11:30, 12:00 noon. There was enough time for the flight attendants to serve lunch. This was back in the days when there was food served on airplanes. It was probably an hour and a half into the flight, and they had virtually completed serving lunch to everybody. There was a jerk and a loud noise. The airplane really lurched. And that was when I knew that obviously there was something wrong.

The pilot was amazingly calm, and the flight attendants were calm. After the plane lurched, it then regained stability, and the flight attendants started picking up the lunch dishes. The pilot came on the PA system shortly after and said, "We've lost an engine. No problem. DC-10s can fly perfectly well on two engines. Sorry for the disturbance. I hope you enjoy the rest of your lunch." Like I said, the flight attendants were picking up the dishes. I noticed that they seemed to be kind of in a hurry, and they weren't offering extra cups of coffee or anything.

It was forty minutes from the time that the plane lurched

until we—I'm going to say "landed" rather than "crashed," because we were intending to land. I think the pilot may have come on two or three times during that time. Again, everybody was calm. There was one member of the flight crew that came back to look out the window. It looked to me, from what I could see, that we were dumping fuel, but I wasn't really sure why he was looking out the window. He was calm. He was congenial, talking to people.

The pilot had told us where we were landing and calmly announced that we would be transported to Chicago—so people making connections would be a little late, but we would get there. So there was confidence that this was just a hitch, that we were going to be fine.

I remember the pilot teaching us what "brace position" means: feet on the floor, your hands on the back of the seat in front of you, and your head down between your knees—and, of course, nothing on your lap. He told us over the PA, "It's going to be the roughest landing you've ever experienced, but we're fine. And when I tell you to brace, I want you to take that position and stay in that position. Don't let go."

And so we were coming in, and I had no visual cues about how close to the ground we were or how far away or anything like that. The only cue I had was the pilot's voice. He yelled, "Brace! Brace! Brace!" And I did. The next thing I was aware of was a huge influx of air and gravel and dirt and debris and stuff hitting me, hitting my face, arms, legs. It was hard to hold on to the seat in front of me. I remember my arms flailing around. I actually grabbed hold of the tie of the man next to me. It was like my body was being bounced around so much I was out of control.

There were at least two periods where I blacked out. When I came to, I remember saying to myself, "Oh, I'm still alive." And then I blacked out again, and then, "Oh, I'm still alive." All this time there was motion and papers and stuff flying around. I had my eyes closed, so I didn't see it, but I could feel it. I don't remember hearing anything other than my own thoughts. And then the motion stopped, and the plane was still.

I wasn't harmed, not physically. Mentally, emotionally, psychologically, I was lightly touched—lightly compared to stories I've heard from other people. I guess I feel fortunate and grateful and in a state of wonder about randomness. You know that so much depends on where somebody was sitting on that plane—just chance.

For me the crash was like a proverbial ocean liner turning around. There were some changes that happened right away, as soon as I got my feet on the ground. And others have unfolded over the sixteen, seventeen years since then.

Immediately, I decided that I wanted to live with as few regrets as possible. And for me that meant repairing relationships that had been compromised and trying very hard not to leave anything undone. So not leaving home in the morning, for example, being upset with someone. Or not passing up a chance to tell Dale, my husband, or one of the boys how much I love them. Or not turning down a chance to tell a friend how much I appreciate her. At first it was very intentional and required a lot of attention. It was hard to do that because it wasn't my habit. But whenever I thought, "Oh, this is hard," then I'd think, "Yeah, well, I might not be coming home tonight. It's not that hard." And it's just turned into a way of being.

What's been longer in unfolding is a reprioritization of my life. At the time this happened, I was traveling on business. I worked hard, and it took a lot of time and a lot of attention. I had worked from the time that my son was in kindergarten. I paid lip service to the notion that my family was my first priority, but when push came to shove, it didn't always work out that way. And so one of the changes that took longer to put into place was to really come down solidly in that value of family first. That took a while longer.

When survivors—especially the survivors that weren't injured very much—were being fed and cared for in Iowa, there were a number of priests and pastors and social workers around. And I ended up talking to a young man who was a social worker, and he said, "God must have had a reason for saving you. You haven't finished your life's work yet." I was quite troubled. It felt to me like I was saddled with a lot of responsibility. "What is this work I'm supposed to be doing that I was saved for?" Part of the struggle was "What is this all about? How do I assign any kind of meaning to this traumatic experience when so many people lost their lives and so many people were severely injured and have never recovered? How do I assign any meaning when I walked out scot-free?"

If you go with that statement, "Well, God has more work for you to do," then the flip side is "God didn't have any more work for all those other people." And I don't believe that. I don't believe in a God that is arbitrary like that and intervenes in our lives in that "destiny" kind of way. What I came to was that there is randomness. There is chance in our world. It impacts all of us in big ways and small ways. And on that day chance impacted me and all the other people on that plane by where you were sitting.

One of the things that has accompanied me, followed me, surrounded me, wrapped me is that feeling of gratitude for whatever happens. That event was like being picked up by the scruff of the neck and shaken. *(Laughter.)* And God says, "This is your only life! Just be grateful for it. *(Crying.)* Just be grateful that you've got these days and these hours and these wonderful people in your life. Just be grateful for that."

June 8, 2006

BLANCA ALVAREZ, 55, interviewed by her daughter, CONNIE ALVAREZ, 33

RECORDED IN SANTA MONICA, CALIFORNIA

Connie Alvarez: When I was little and I heard pieces of the story of how you crossed from Mexico, I used to hear you guys talk about a coyote, and I didn't understand that that's what you call the people who crossed you. For the longest time when I was growing up I thought you were running with real coyotes in the desert, and they somehow were able to bring you over and carry me safely into the United States. So I thought that I had a special connection with coyotes. But now I know what a coyote means. What was the journey like?

Blanca Alvarez: We were walking and walking. For me it was an eternity. I don't know how long. I didn't have a watch with me or anything. He told us to take our shoes off. He said, "I don't want no noise because the dogs are very, very good to detect every noise." And he said, "I'm going to whistle when the border patrol change shifts." He told us two different kind of whistles that he was going to make. He said, "When I whistle like this, you're going to duck, and when I whistle like this, you're going to run."

He whistled, so we went on our stomachs and we stayed there. Oh my God, I could see big ants crawling, and I was so scared. Because I was very scared and I wanted to go back, my cousin told me, "Don't worry. It's not going to take us that long." So when he whistled again, we stood up and we ran. He told us, "Run right now! Run!" I remember it was torture on those rocks without shoes. So we ran as fast as we could, and then he said, "Put your shoes on right here."

We were at kind of like a bridge, and he said, "You're going to walk over that bridge. I'm going to walk behind you, and you're going to put your hand behind and give me the money there. There's a post office. You go in the post office, and if you have money, buy stamps. And then from there you're on your own."

Connie: Why do you think he wanted you to buy stamps?

Blanca: I don't know. Probably because he didn't want them to think we were crossing the border. I don't know. There was a telephone booth, and I called a taxi to get to your aunt's house. I wasn't sure if I had enough money to pay for the taxi, but my cousin did. And, besides, I couldn't walk anymore because of the rocks.

We went through a lot of things—like, for example, not eating. For six months your father lost his job, and we never told you that. I guess because we never want to worry you.

Connie: I do remember a lot of beans, bean tacos. And I had to wear boys hand-me-downs. What kinds of jobs did you have?

Blanca: We were gardeners. And we were cleaning offices.

Connie: I remember the offices. I remember being with my brother in our pajamas with the little plastic feet, and I have memories of running into everyone's office and eating candy from their candy dishes. You used to put us to bed on people's office couches while you worked all night.

Blanca: You remember that?

Connie: And I also remember you would always buy us a Cup o' Noodle from the vending machine, like a snack, a soup snack, and then put us to bed, and then you'd carry us to the car when you guys were done cleaning the offices. I remember that. How old was I when you decided to go back to school here in the U.S.?

Blanca: I guess you were nine years old when I went to high school and then went to college, and then went to university. I was so busy going to school that I guess I neglected you a little bit.

Connie: No. Because for me, watching you go to school with two kids and trying to make ends meet—that was the biggest inspiration for me to finish college. I felt there was no way that I couldn't finish if you could do it with all of that. Even when I wanted to drop out, I thought there's nothing that could stand in my way that didn't stand in yours more. So there was no neglect there. You don't have to worry about that.

Blanca: You never told me you felt like that.

Connie: It's the most important thing for me, having gone to college. And I feel like anything I do from here on out is okay, because I have already achieved my dream of getting a college degree. Everything else is icing on the cake.

January 9, 2006

EDDIE S. LANIER JR., 60, interviewed
by his friend DAVID WRIGHT, 51

RECORDED IN DURHAM, NORTH CAROLINA

Eddie S. Lanier Jr.: My daddy was elected mayor of Chapel
Hill twice. That's where I got my nickname. I used to walk
down the streets holding his hand on Main Street, and
everybody'd stop, pet me on the head, and say, "How you
doing, Little Mayor?" (*Laughs.*)

I had chronic alcoholism on both sides of my family,
Mother's and Daddy's. But the worst came out of my daddy's
side. My daddy came up from Georgia, a farmer. Everybody
made white liquor down there, and he was raised up in that
mess. And he had five brothers. He was the oldest. And I
guess he had some help from God because all of my uncles
and my grandfather died either accidental deaths related to
alcoholism or directly from alcoholism. Daddy saw what
it had done to them and just said to himself, "This is not
going to be."

When I was about fourteen, he said, "I want to have a talk
with you." I said, "Okay, Daddy. What is it?" And he said,
"Son, look, you come from a long line of chronic alcoholics.
They're all dead now except for me. And the only reason I'm
not dead is because I recognized that it was in the genes. I was
an alcoholic just waiting for the first drink, and I refused to take
it." He said, "If you do take that drink you'll get away with it

for a while, but it'll catch you fast. And it's going to destroy your life and probably kill you." And he said, "I want you to remember that as you get older." I said, "Okay, Daddy. I'll give it serious thought."

I gave it enough thought that that Halloween I went trick-or-treating with my buddy here in Chapel Hill, and we passed a horseshoe of frat houses. It was a warm Halloween night, and they were all out and partying. Those kids knew who I was. Everybody knew who my daddy was, and one of them frat boys said, "Hey, you ever had a drink?" And I said, "No." I hadn't. So they poured me a double shot of 100-proof Smirnoff vodka. He said, "Now you drink this. Hold your breath and take this water. It's going to burn," he said, "but you're going to like it." So I did it, you know, on an empty stomach. I was fourteen and about ninety pounds.

I never felt so good in my life. Oh, God—it was Dr. Jekyll and Mr. Hyde! I had found the solution to all my problems. I was this very skinny child, and I didn't fit in. I had low self-esteem. Even though my daddy was who he was, that didn't help because all the kids would say, "Screw him and his daddy," and the bullies picked on me and took my lunch money. And I was clumsy. I was one of them guys that when the two captains picked teams and it'd get down to me, they'd have to fight over which one was going to get me, because this guy's a disaster. Two left feet, couldn't dance, scared of girls. Everybody knew.

The next morning on the way to school I stopped right through that frat house where the boys had the party. There was liquor everywhere. I got some right quick. And when I got out there on the playground, there stood the arch bully of Chapel Hill Elementary School: Billy Blake, the chief of police's son. He weighed about 180 pounds. Big kid. But things had changed. I didn't wait for him to take my lunch money. I just beat him senseless. I broke his nose, knocked out three of his teeth. I wasn't scared of anything or anybody anymore.

Then I became the school bully. I grew my hair long. Girls started taking an interest in me. I went to sock hops. I could dance. My grades improved. I wasn't scared of public speaking, like when you give a book report. I just found the answer to all my problems. And I hung with that magic elixir for forty-some more years of my life. As long as I had alcohol in my system, I was what I always wanted to be: a self-confident, good-looking, intelligent, sharp, witty human being. And it worked very well until time took its toll and my daddy's words came into play.

David Wright: Must take a lot of self-discipline to turn around.

Eddie: Well, it took more than that. I had just been released from my twenty-eighth treatment for alcoholism. My last drunk was in Durham, and I had reached a point where my body was rejecting the alcohol. It was a catch-22. I had to have it, but I couldn't get it down. And I knew I was going to have an alcoholic seizure and die. On the day of my discharge, I came into the doctor's office. They all looked at me with not a smile. I sat down there, and the doctor said, "Mr.

Lanier, I've dedicated my life to helping alcoholics." He said, "I came from a family that was destroyed by it. I could be making lots more money than I'm making now, but this is my purpose." He said, "Listen to me: Your blood work is such a mess, you should be dead." He said, "Every bit of your liver is hard, except a place the size of a twenty-five-cent piece. When you leave here, I'm going to read your name in the obituaries in less than two weeks, because that's all the time you've got left if you start drinking again. And I know you will. Good luck."

So I went to Chapel Hill, and I stopped at the cemetery where my mother and daddy were buried. I let them know that I had had my last drink, and I was going to die sober. And I wanted to apologize for all the misery I put them through, and that if they didn't get the message directly, I'd appreciate, God, if you'd tell them that I'm sober and going to die this way.

I had lost my ID on my last drunk, so I couldn't even prove who I was; I couldn't get a job. That was in April of 2001. So then I came on down to a place I knew was safe and set up a camp. I went out on the bypass where there's an exit ramp off of Raleigh Road. They had a traffic island there, and I held up a sign: "Homeless. Anything will help. God bless."

And that's where I met you. Every time you came by, you'd stick out a two-dollar bill and a can of tuna fish. So I'd say, "Oh, boy. The two-dollar-bill man." I think it was probably obvious to you that I wasn't drinking with the money. Anyway, that's how we met.

One New Year's Eve I had no family, nowhere to go. And you walked on over and said, "Remember me?" I said, "Yeah—you're the two-dollar-bill man." You said, "I'm going to take you home with me for New Year's Eve. How would you like that?" I said, "I don't think that would work, sir. I'm dirty. I stink. I haven't had a bath. Look at me." I said, "You got a wife?" "Yeah, I got a wife and a little daughter." I said, "I don't think she's going to have too much to say about bringing a homeless, smelly old man home with you." And you said, "My wife will receive you well."

I was skeptical, but I went to your home and had a shower, and you gave me some clean clothes. And I came out and met your wife and little daughter. And your wife was so nice. We had lots of things in common that we got to talk about. We had a wonderful time. We sat down at the table, and I told you some stories about who I really was and who my daddy was. There was a lot more to me than you might have imagined.

David: I hope I was a little bit of a help along your path, and I want to thank you for being a good role model to me.

Eddie: Well, you know, David, you made it much easier to stay sober. Without you, the kindness of your family, letting me come home with you with a smile, and giving me a pat on the back and a shower—I don't know. I wouldn't say I'd have gone back drinking again, but I'd say it would have been rough.

April 15, 2006

Eddie S. Lanier Jr. (l.) and
David Wright (r.)

PAUL MORTIMER, 49, and
SHAWN FOX, 39, interview each other

RECORDED IN SALEM, OREGON

In October 2005, StoryCorps was invited inside the Oregon State Penitentiary to record a series of interviews with inmates and staff.

Paul Mortimer: My name is Paul Mortimer. My friends call me Bumper. I'm forty-nine years old. We're at the Oregon State Penitentiary. I'm talking to a good friend of mine named Shawn Fox. Tell me about your childhood.

Shawn Fox: I was born and raised right here in Salem, Oregon. A large family—eight kids, five sisters and two brothers. I'm second to the youngest. My baby sister died in 2002 of cancer. The rest of the kids are all still living. Most of them are drug addicts. Their lives are pretty shot.

Paul: What started your life of crime?

Shawn: I would hang out with my older brother from the time I was probably about five or six. I wanted to be with him all the time. I think it started there. He could push me through the window of the neighbor's house. I'd go in, unlock the door for him. "Come here. Smoke a little weed with me. Don't tell Momma." So that probably started it. He robbed some paperboy, knocked him down, took his money, and went to MacLaren Youth Authority, and I just kept on doing stuff by myself.

Paul: When was the first time you were locked up?

Shawn: At age eleven. I broke into the neighbor's house—they were weed dealers. I'd watch 'em out the window and see where their key was, get in their house, and steal a little weed. I ended up taking somebody with me, and he was older, and he wanted to steal the whiskey and guns, and they reported it. They sent me to the boys' home for a year. Saint Mary's Boys' Home in Beaverton, Oregon. That's where it all went downhill.

Paul: What's your present offense?

Shawn: Aggravated murder.

Paul: What's your sentence?

Shawn: Double consecutive life without the possibility of parole. It was a single gunshot wound to the guy's temple. It was an accident; it was a struggle over a gun.

Paul: Drug related?

Shawn: Yeah. He was a Mexican national selling dope in a motel. I went in there to rob him, and he slapped the pistol away from his face, and it discharged and killed him instantly. A piece of his head flew right in my mouth, you know. Phoo! Spit that out. I didn't even pick up the dope, it startled me so bad. I just ran out of there. It was right in the temple, so they said that I executed him. I didn't help my attorneys with the trial. They could say whatever because I remained quiet. And they gave me a double consecutive life without parole.

My little boy come in here when he was five—he just turned twelve—and he said, "Daddy, please come home for just a little while." I told him, "I can't, buddy." He ran to the door and put his head down, crying. He thought I was rejecting him. My daughter when she was thirteen—she's sixteen now—she said to her momma, "Dad must not really love us. If he did, he wouldn't have left us out here like this." I get up every day and look in that mirror and I think of that. And that right there, that'll make you want to turn to drugs. Who wants to face that?

Paul: What are your hopes for your kids?

Shawn: I don't want 'em to get locked up. My dad spent eleven years in prison. Both my brothers were in prison. I get up every day, and I pray that my kids don't wind up here—that none of my boys or my daughter start smoking weed. I worry about that. It's just normal kid stuff in school, and it would be all right if it was just that. But I know what it ends up leading to.

Paul: Exactly. I mean when I first got high, I fell in love with it. That was the love of my life. I was probably eleven or twelve years old when I first got high smoking weed. Then ran into some pills and started taking those, and that was a better high and fell in love with that even more. And one step led to the next, chasing that dragon. And it does nothing. All they do is wind you up in these places. Don't know no successful drug addicts. None. I'm forty-nine years old. I've been here almost twenty-one years for drug-related robbery. And for what? A little bit of money?

I was born in Detroit, Michigan. My parents moved to California before I was a year old, and I grew up in a middle-class family. There were six of us kids. And I had an average middle-class upbringing till my parents separated. Then things just went real sour. As soon as my father left, it was on. My mom worked as a registered nurse trying to make all the house payments. She didn't have time to keep an eye on us, so we took advantage of that.

I went through the same thing you did. Start out in juvenile halls and work my way through boys' homes, then the youth authority, then wound up in the joint down in Arizona. Came up here and wound up in this place, and been here ever since. Drug habit's continued ever since. I don't know what it'll take to stop. I've been clean a year, and that's the first time I've been clean since I've been here, and I've been here almost twenty-one years. I've been dirty pretty much the whole time.

I met my wife, Nettie, in here in 1990 over the telephone. A friend of mine asked me if I wanted to talk to a friend of his. We started writing as friends, and we just kept writing, and one thing turned into another. She started coming to visit. Realized I loved her, asked her to marry me in the visiting room, and she said yes. We've been together ever since. She's missed maybe five visits in fifteen years. I've tried to run her off. I've OD'd in here four times, and I tried to tell her just to leave, I don't need to drag you down. But she ain't going nowhere; she don't want to hear it. I told her, "I ain't coming out to see you." She says, "I'll just come up every visit until you come out." I tell her I'm not going to write anymore, and she says, "I'm going to write you until you write me." So what can you

say to that? She's my buddy, you know. My life. I believe, I seriously believe, that if it wasn't for her, I would probably have
gave up a long time ago and done something really horrendous
in here.

This place is monotonous. Every day the same thing. You
go outside, and if you're into lifting weights, you go lift weights.
Then what? The rest of your day is dead.

Shawn: The boredom is huge. Huge. Same stuff over and
over every day. Go sit on the bench. . . .

Paul: Walk a few laps.

Shawn: Better go write a letter. Okay, it's time to eat dinner. That's it. Over and over for years and years. No gum, no
women, no kids.

Paul: No dogs, no cats.

Shawn: No swimming. Things people take for granted. I
would love to mow a lawn.

Paul: The smell of it. When them trash trucks come in
with the exhaust, most people don't want to smell that. I try
to get a noseful of it, because it brings back memories of being
on the streets. I mean, if you think about it, that is *sorry*. I
mean, that's the highlight of your day—getting a noseful of
exhaust? But, you know, that's the reality of being in prison.
And the really messed-up part about it is I put myself here. I'm
guilty of the charges I'm here for. I can't blame nobody but the
person I look at in the mirror every day.

Shawn: Think you'll ever get out?

Paul: Yeah, I do. I see the parole board every two years, and
if I can leave the drugs alone long enough, I'll get a date. I'll

probably be fifty-five, close to sixty, when I get out. But I will get back out.

October 17, 2005

Paul Mortimer died of a drug overdose on November 11, 2005, less than a month after this interview was recorded.

Paul Mortimer (l.) and
Shawn Fox (r.)

* * * * * * * * * * *

JOHN BROWN, 36, interviewed by his brother PAUL CORBIT BROWN, 39

RECORDED IN CHARLESTON, WEST VIRGINIA

Paul Corbit Brown: How was it for you coming out?

John Brown: Well, I guess there were three coming-out stories: when I came out to you, when I came out to Danny, and when I came out to Mom. I don't remember ever coming out to Dad.

I remember when I came out to you, you just said, "Oh, I've known since you were nine. What took you so long?" You were very flippant about it, in a very reassuring way. It was okay. And that was really good for me that it was very no-nonsense. When I came out to Danny, it was very different. We're driving down Court Street in Charleston, and I said, "Danny, I need to tell you something." And he's like, "Okay," and I said, "You're going to hear it from someone eventually, and I want you to hear it from me. I'm gay." And he just starts bawling and crying. I mean just these great, old, big crocodile tears. And I said, "What is it, man? It's not that bad, honestly." *(Laughter.)* I was probably seventeen years old. And he said, "It's all my fault! It's all my fault! It's all my fault!" I said, "How in the world can it be your fault?" And just in this incredible moment of clarity he looks at me, and he wipes the big tears out of his eyes, and he says, "I've called you cocksucker all these years!" And I said, "Oh, Danny, if that's all it took, half the people in town would have been gay." *(Laughter.)* You know, that's his favorite phrase and always has been. So, you know, it was a bonding moment for Danny and me. And you know, of course, when I told Mom, I think she cried for three weeks.

Paul: Maybe longer.

John: Maybe longer. Which I never really understood and couldn't quite get my hands around. But I don't know. Growing up, the hardest part for me was sitting in that pew and listening to people tell me how bad I was, you know?

Paul: So when did you find your voice?

John: I guess I found my literal voice in 1993. I had made an incredible journey to get to the march on Washington, one of the major lesbian and gay marches. And once I got there, it was just wonderful to be around all those folks who I had something in common with. And then the next morning, when I returned home, I was driving to work scanning through the stations, and I landed on WJYP, Joy and Praise 101 or something, a Christian broadcasting station. And the announcer was saying all these terrible things about the march. And so I pulled off the side of the road, and I went to a pay phone, and I called the station. And they put him on the phone, and I said, "What are you thinking?" I said, "Were you there? Did you attend this event? You talk about it on the radio as if you were there. You weren't there. I was there." I said, "If you're going to talk about gay and lesbian people, you should have somebody gay or lesbian on the show." "Oh, we've tried really hard. We've tried many times to get somebody on the show." And I said, "I'll be on your show." And he said, "No, you won't. People say that, but they won't show up." And I said, "You tell me the time and the place, and I'll be there."

And he said, "Well, it's ten of seven. We're going to have a live segment at seven-thirty if you want to be here. We'll put you on the show for ten minutes." And I said, "Okay." So I hung up the phone. And, of course, I was shaking. I mean, I was absolutely trembling. And I went to the Hardee's across the street, and I got five dollars in quarters, and I called everybody I knew, and I said, "You've got to call in to this show, because I'm absolutely petrified."

So, at any rate, I got up there, and we were in this little studio, and I remember there was just a bare lightbulb hanging down from the ceiling. That was it. And in behind me walked this really big guy. But it was amazing. Once I sat down, I was just as comfortable as I could be. And we went through the first fifteen minutes, and he said to me, "I'm sure you won't want to stay." And I said, "No, I'm perfectly comfortable. I'll sit here until you're ready to turn off the microphone." And we sat there for another two and a half hours and talked about these issues. Even though 99.9 percent of the callers who called in to that show just talked about me like I was a dog, about how sick and perverted it was, that didn't matter. What mattered is that there was somebody out there in that audience who was listening, who needed to hear that I was gay and they were gay and it was okay. That was the only person I was worried about. The rest of those people didn't matter at all to me. And that's how I try to live my life.

Paul: When I think about you, I think about the way that you, like Dad, very much walk your talk. And I really admire that—hugely. Because I don't know very many people like you. And I mean it when I say that you're one of the most important people in my life. I think that my relationship with you has had one of the most profound effects on who I am as a person.

John: In my life, as things have progressed, I've found it to be a great honor to have you and Danny for brothers 'cause you've been probably two of the most important people in my life. I talk about you all the time. And a lot of times my friends will say, "I can't even talk to my brother about the weather." And I say, "I tell my brothers everything." (*Laughter.*) It's great for me to have you and Danny as my brothers. I really love you both.

June 26, 2005

*Paul Corbit Brown (l.) and
John Brown (r.)*

KIM SCHUMER, 18, interviewed
by her sister, AMY SCHUMER, 22
RECORDED IN NEW YORK CITY

Amy Schumer: Kim, what's your first memory?

Kim Schumer: I have a memory of my fifth birthday, which is kind of random. Jumping on Mom's bed in a lion nightgown and being really excited that it was my fifth birthday because five's a pretty big year for a kid. That was probably my first memory.

Amy: What's your first memory of me?

Kim: My first memory of you is us dancing in the living room, probably to "Footloose." I remember dancing and jumping on the couch and thinking that we were the greatest dancers alive, which we probably were.

Amy: What's your memory of the most afraid you've ever been?

Kim: The most afraid I've ever been is probably when I went to the hospital for the first time. I was in the psych ward for adolescents, and I was in my bed, and the roommate that I got put with was just bouncing-off-the-walls crazy. It was mainly for people with drug and violence problems, but that wasn't why I was there.

Amy: Why were you there?

Kim: At that point I was actively cutting myself—self-mutilation. It got to a point where Mom was scared and my therapist was scared and I was scared. So I went to the hospital. And I was scared because I was lying in bed and I looked at my roommate, and she was just telling me stories about horrible things that she'd done to herself, like trying to throw herself out the window, trying to cut her wrist with nail clippers. And the scary thing was that I knew that that's exactly where I was heading. And so that was probably the scariest—when I realized that that was the path I was on.

Amy: Who first noticed it and said something to you about your arms being cut?

Kim: Oh, God—my volleyball coach. I was at practice, and I had a Band-Aid over my wrist, because I used to get up in the morning, go to school, leave after an hour of school, come home and cut myself, sleep for a few hours, and then go back to volleyball practice because I love volleyball. And my coach saw the Band-Aid because I was playing; I was sweating, and it slipped off. And she pulled me into the locker room, and she grabbed my arms and she said, "Kim, what are you doing to yourself?" And I lost it. Like I just— I was hysterically crying. And I was like, "It's nothing. It's the cat." And she's like, "It's not the cat. A cat doesn't leave this." And that's when I told my mom. She flipped out. And I was like, "Note to self: Don't tell Mom again."

But after you do it a few times, it feels so good, and it's just easy to keep doing it. So that's when people started noticing. It wasn't until the first time I tried to stop that I realized how addicted to it I was, because I would be in the shower and I would get an urge to do it and I would be like, "Okay, I'm not going to do it." And I would get sick and throw up. And my arm would start tingling, and like—

Amy: Withdrawal.

Kim: I would go through physical withdrawal from it. That's how I knew that it was a problem, because when I tried to stop, I physically couldn't.

Amy: I didn't understand the severity of it until one time we went to Florida to visit our grandmother. And you were trying to not cut yourself anymore, and you got an urge to. You got up from watching *Saturday Night Live* and went upstairs to take a hot shower. And I said, "Mom, what's wrong with Kim?" She said, "She just has an urge. She wants to cut herself." And then I heard noises upstairs. I didn't understand that your body gets addicted to cutting itself, like worse than heroin. And I walked toward the stairs, and I saw my mom going upstairs with a razor. And I said, "What the hell are you doing, Mom?" And she said, "You don't understand. You have to let me by." And I was like, "There is no way I'm letting you bring a razor up to my little sister." And she said I didn't understand. The psychologist said you have to give it to her because she'll use something else. She'll break her head on a mirror and use pieces of the mirror.

I went up to you. You were in the shower and just beside yourself. I said, "Kim, you don't have to do this." And you were just cursing at me and screaming, "You have no idea what it's like!" And it was like another person. It was like *The Exorcist.* And I just— I said, "You don't have to do this," and I left. And I was just comatose. I couldn't believe it. And then ten minutes later Mom kind of threw the razor down the stairs, and she yelled, "She didn't use it! She didn't use it!" And I think that was like the hardest but the best. And I was the most proud of you I've ever been, because I didn't really understand how difficult it is to fight off that kind of an urge.

What are you the most proud of?

Kim: I'm most proud of stopping cutting myself. Next month, on the twenty-second, it'll be three years since I've cut myself. Tomorrow is my thirty-five-month anniversary. I know how many days it is. It's still on my mind all the time. But I'm most proud of it because it was the hardest thing that I've ever had to do, and it continues to be the hardest thing that I do— or not do, for that matter.

Amy: What made you stop cutting yourself?

Kim: I don't know. I did a lot of reading on it. And therapy— My therapist is the best, and she has helped me so much. I'm really big on logic and rationality with things, and I kind of realized that I'm not going to be able to keep cutting myself. Like physically, I am not going to be able to. It'll just get worse and worse, because every time I cut, I would have to cut deeper. So I would either have to stop cutting myself or kill myself. And it kind of went from there.

Amy: And why can you never kill yourself?

Kim: Because you'll kick my ass. (*Laughter.*) I've been real close to committing suicide two times in my life. And both times the only reason that I didn't is because of you and because of Mom. And I could never, ever do that to either of you, because no matter how bad things get with me, I love you more than I need to be temporarily happy. So while it seemed like the only option, I couldn't do it.

Amy: Because I would die.

Kim: I know.

Amy: Thank you. I love you.

Kim: I love you so much!

November 21, 2003

*Kim (l.) and
Amy (r.) Schumer*

CURTIS CATES, 54, interviewed by his wife, CINDY CONNOLLY CATES, 47

RECORDED IN NEW YORK CITY

Curtis Cates: I was born and raised in Lubbock, Texas, but my father was a truck driver, so we tended to move around Texas quite a bit. I adored my father. He was a classic cowboy. It was like growing up around a TV star. Sometimes he would park the truck in our neighborhood, and to me it was the equivalent of putting a prize stallion in your front yard. It was like the proudest thing in the world was to have that truck in our front yard.

Cindy Connolly Cates: What was it like to be in the truck with your dad?

Curtis: My dad would take speed, so he sang a lot and he talked a lot, and then he would always fool around with the waitresses in all the truck stops that we stopped at. We hauled everything from grain to dynamite to a lot of cotton. Maybe we'd be in twenty states in the summer, so when I'd get back to school, it'd be like, "What did you do on your summer vacation?" It was a joke, because I'd just spent two months in a truck going all over the country.

Cindy: You idolized your father.

Curtis: Well, I mean, I didn't have any choice in the matter. When it came to buying clothes, my father and I would buy exactly the same clothes down to a hat—you know, a

Western hat and boots and Levi's and the whole bit. He was a very bright man, and he was a very unusual and charismatic, extremely handsome guy.

Cindy: So how would you describe yourself as a child?

Curtis: I thought I was happy. It's interesting, but it's only in time that I've come to realize that my childhood was not what I thought it was when it was happening. I felt like a happy-go-lucky kid, a normal kid. But looking back at things, I don't think I was as happy as I thought I was. I look back, and my father was gone all the time. When he would come home, him and my mother would fight. I had to spend all my summers and holidays in the truck with my father, and he was a womanizer, and he was addicted to speed, and he would drive the truck four and five days at a time without stopping, and it was a lot of weird drama of my mother catching him with other women. So I think that I isolated myself in this make-believe world, which is probably a very common thing with children.

Cindy: What's your greatest accomplishment in life on a personal level?

Curtis: I think getting married, having a home, having a sense of normalcy in my life, working on overcoming my addiction to heroin, just trying to be a normal guy.

Cindy: It's so funny to listen to you because you sound so serious. I mean, I've heard all these stories, of course, but you sound like the most serious person in the world, and anyone who knows you knows that you're an absolutely hilarious, fun person. Do you think that people have a different perception of you?

Curtis: I think there's a perception that I'm this funny guy that's not serious about anything, and it serves me well as a coat of armor, when inside I'm actually pretty banged up.

Cindy: Right. I see that person at home.

Curtis: I know that my real feelings—the feelings that make up the core of my personality—are not happy. I mean, it's weird. I'll start bawling at the strangest times. I might be watching *Bonanza* and start crying because Little Joe was mean to Hoss.

Cindy: Has our marriage helped you at all?

Curtis: Yes. Absolutely. Tremendously. I found my life's partner. I found my soul mate. I knew that you were good for me when you said one day that we were just two tortured mutts. That was the day I knew that I wanted to marry you.

Cindy: That's so sad.

Curtis: But that's exactly how I feel. I feel like a tortured mutt, so I knew if you were a tortured mutt and I was a tortured mutt, then we could probably give each other love.

December 3, 2005

GEORGE CAYWOOD, 67, interviewed by his daughter GINA CAYWOOD, 38

RECORDED IN SANTA MONICA, CALIFORNIA

George Caywood: My dad was raised on a farm in Oklahoma and could do just about anything, but he couldn't do any specific thing well enough to be a real professional. So we were desperately poor and frequently hungry. There was often no money to buy laundry soap to wash my clothes, and so my clothes were always dirty. I had four sisters and one brother. I was the fifth child; I have a younger sister. However, my role in the family was to keep everything sane enough that everyone could grow up. So I took care of everyone.

Gina Caywood: I know one of the things that was extremely difficult for you was when your father committed suicide. So can you tell me about that? (*Crying.*)

George: Sure. He was bipolar, and he went into a down episode, a really severe down episode. I was fifteen. And he came to me one day and asked me where I kept my gun. I'd gotten a .22 from my uncle the previous Christmas, and I had it broken down with the bullets stored in a separate place. I thought he was worried about my little sister getting ahold of the gun. I was really encouraged. I thought that meant he was coming out of his depression.

I went to Tucson to my uncle's wedding, and while I was gone, he took my gun and shot himself through the head. My job was to take care of other people, so what I was feeling, I didn't pay any attention to it. I have no idea what I was think-ing other than "What can I say to Aunt Laura to help her calm down?" "What can I say to Aunt Nellie? Can I hug her? Can I give her a kiss?" I was kind of programmed to take care of everyone.

So when I was fifteen—and just a few days after my dad had shot himself with my gun—at his funeral, I remember going from adult to adult, comforting them. And it seemed appropriate to me. And from that day to this, Gina, nobody who was an adult ever asked me how I felt about having my dad . . . (Crying.)

Gina: Use your gun to kill himself?

George: Yeah.

Gina: And how do you feel about it?

George: Ten or so years ago, a friend of mine died, and he had teenage children. I was sitting in the church, just watch-ing the adults come in and just love the teenagers in the fam-ily. And that was the first time in my life I ever realized how inappropriate it was that no one comforted me. It just wasn't done in our family.

Gina: And so how did you feel about your dad using your gun to kill himself?

George: I felt horribly guilty, just unspeakably guilty, be-cause I gave him my gun. I felt like I had killed my dad.

Gina: And how is it that you, with such a difficult child-hood, were such a wonderful, loving father to us?

George: I've done a lot of things in my life that I value, but nothing more than being the father of my four daughters. And I remember when you were born, Gina, looking at you, at this beautiful little baby, saying, "I have no idea how to be your father." And I said, "What I'm going to do is read the Bible." The Bible is what I had growing up. So I began to read the Bible, and I discovered in the Bible that God has two primary characteristics in terms of being a father: God was flexible and merciful. So I set out to be as flexible and as merciful as I possibly could be.

And I wanted you to have a fun childhood. I knew I was going to have to say no, but I wanted your experience to be one *no* against thousands of *yeses* in the hopes that you would grow up as positive as you actually are.

Gina: And I know sometimes when you did say no, I could bat my eyelashes at you and get you to change your mind.

George: It still works. Each of the four girls had their own technique. Yours was those brown eyes. See, I'm melting on the spot! (*Laughs.*) And Jill was just so everlastingly on my side that she was hard to resist, because she was always working for my benefit, and Janelle, who turned out to be a very capable attorney, remembered everything I ever said—date and time. And she would say, "Now, Dad, four years ago on this date you said this, and now you're saying this. Don't you think you're being inconsistent?" And then JoAnna was so sure she was right that she would grab my face between her hands and turn me to look at her, sort of saying, "My dad is an understanding person. He's reasonably bright. If I could just get him to see the truth, he'll surely let me do what I want!" So you all had your techniques, and they all worked. And oh, boy, the four of you together—I just gave up. I knew I was whipped. (*Laughs.*)

Gina: You know, Dad, one of the most difficult times in my childhood was when we were all in our teens, and you went through a major depression. And the father before the depression was a wonderful father. But then you went through this dark period. Can you tell me what that was like?

George: Well, if you've ever been walking down the street, maybe at night, and a huge dog charges you growling and barking—that moment of utter panic and fear—it's like that twenty hours a day. All this stuff that I've talked about here was so unpleasant and painful, and most of it was bottled up inside of me. And I knew that if I was going to be genuinely happy, which I wanted to be, I was going to have to face all that darkness. So I prayed many times: "God, I know this stuff has to come up." And it's up, Gina. I have peace in my deepest heart. Sometimes I say, "I own my own belly now." Nothing is going to jump out from behind some wall to scare me. I've faced all of it.

Gina: I remember one of the hardest times for me was our bedrooms had a common wall, and I could hear at four in the morning, five in the morning, you crying. Just terrified to go to work and to take on another day.

George: Do you remember the poem you wrote me?

Gina: I do. It was "Jesus, Can I Have My Dad Back?" During that time I would think longingly of the days predepression. I'd remember you laughing and us going camping and all the fun stuff that we did. And then to see you crying and terrified and, you know, suicidal yourself was so difficult. And it's amazing, once that was behind us, you are today an enormously different person.

George: I loved you with all my life, but so much of my

heart was locked up in fear and guilt and remorse that I—
There just wasn't a lot left for love. But you have not breathed
a breath, Gina, you and your sisters, when you weren't the
most important thing in my life.

Gina: You worked in a rescue mission on skid row here in
L.A. for almost twenty years. And I know we grew up visiting
that mission once or twice a week. We developed very good
friendships with the men who'd been on the street. And I've
heard you say numerous times when people give you accolades
for working with the homeless, you always say, "These men,
women, and children gave me more than I could ever give
in return."

George: Absolutely.

Gina: Can you tell me an example?

George: I was in my office. I wasn't fully out of my depression, and your mother and I were well on our way to divorce. Working like crazy, exhausted, probably eight o'clock
at night, and I was so lonely. I used to get a haircut once a
week just to have someone touch me. And I'm sitting in my
office and I said, "God, I need you to touch my arm. I need
you to physically touch my arm." And I just sat there praying,
hoping something would happen—but of course nothing did.
So I walked down this huge flight of stairs just feeling miser-
able. I walked out the front door to the left to go to the parking lot. And I'd spent a lot of time walking in the streets, just
talking to people, including women who were street prosti-
tutes. And I never hugged the women because they had been
so abused by men that they just didn't want to be touched.
Most of the time I didn't even try to shake their hands. So

here I am, my heart just broken. And I look up the street, maybe twenty-five yards away, there's this woman I knew to be a street prostitute. She took one look at me—it was like the movies, Gina—she started running towards me and threw her arms open, threw her arms around me, and kissed me on the cheek, and then just went on. And I was so shocked. And in some way it really transformed my view of God, because God did not pick a religious person or a business executive. Here's this woman, forty or so, probably had AIDS, her front teeth were knocked out because someone thought it was better for oral sex, and that's who God chose to physically touch me. And somehow that seemed so fitting.

Gina: You know, Dad, you really have had an amazing life and a lot of difficulty and a lot of tragedy, and yet today you're the happiest person I know. You live a very simple life. You're not a wealthy man; you don't have a lot of personal possessions—all those things that people think we need to have to be happy—and yet you're so happy.

George: I've worked hard, Gina. I've worked hard at being healthy, and I certainly have a lot of support.

Gina: I know that you were asked to leave the mission, because they were a very conservative Christian organization, and you fought not to require everybody to sit through a service so they could get food, and to bring recovery programs to the mission. I think one of the things that my sisters and I always felt devastated about is that you are a great, great man and have done— (Crying.) You have made such a contribution to society, and yet you've never had your day of honor.

George: Oh, Gina, I'm having it right now.

Gina: Well, that's—and I didn't want to tell you this in advance—but that's part of why I wanted to do this today, is to— You know my sisters and I, they know that I'm doing this to give you the honor that we felt that you never got. *(Crying.)* I told you I was going to lose it.

George: Let's just sit here and cry for a minute. *(Laughter.)*

Gina: There's so many people that you've touched. You've fought for social justice, and you've taken the time to talk and love and care and support people. And it's definitely your gift, and I hope somehow this interview today with StoryCorps gives you the honor that I think you deserve.

George: I wouldn't trade this for every accolade in the world.

Gina: Thanks, Dad.

George: I love you, honey.

Gina: I love you, too.

January 14, 2006

SHASTI O'LEARY-SOUDANT, 39,
interviewed by her husband,
JETHRO SOUDANT, 34

RECORDED IN NEW YORK CITY

Shasti O'Leary-Soudant: The happiest and the worst day of
my life were the same day. I was about five months into chemo,
and I was getting really sick. The moment that we walked off
the elevator, I started feeling nauseous. They'd have to take me
into the back room, because they couldn't give it to me with
all the other patients. And the moment that the needle punc-
tured the skin, I threw up. You were ready for it. You caught it.
I soiled myself. I couldn't control any of my bodily functions. I
was crying hysterically. And you said something that made me
laugh. And I still can't remember what it was. You were just
looking at me right in the eye, and you said something really
funny. It was something about how I looked or that you loved
me, or it was just like you were radiating love out of your face
at me. It was like shining a light on me. I felt like I was looking into the sun. And it was the most incredible moment of my
life because I had no doubt—I just had this perfect moment of
certainty—that you loved me. And I knew that there was nothing that would take you, there was nothing that would take me.
If I died, it would never stop. If you died, it would continue. I
thought about our vows. It was the most incredible moment because you can't think of being in any worse shape than I was at
that exact second except that I was laughing.

Jethro Soudant: That's when you kind of broke. That was probably the lowest point but became the highest point.

Shasti: I guess I just sort of let it happen from that point on. I let you take care of me. And that was a long slog. That was a fight. But all of a sudden I just felt no matter what happened, everything was going to be fine.

January 14, 2006

GREGG KORBON, 57, speaks to his wife, KATHRYN KORBON, 52

RECORDED IN CHARLOTTESVILLE, VIRGINIA

Gregg Korbon: There's a Little League baseball field in Charlottesville called Brian C. Korbon Field, and I would like to tell the story of how it got its name. The story goes back twelve years ago when our son Brian was getting ready for his ninth birthday. He started having difficulties sleeping, and he said that he did not want to celebrate his birthday. He said celebrating his birthday would bring his death, and he would never make it to double digits, meaning ten years old. We didn't understand that, because he was healthy. He had had heart surgery when he was a little baby, but that had gone well, and the doctors told us that we really didn't have anything to worry about.

He was a very bright little boy, and we were just beginning to have him tested to see if he was gifted. He was having trouble fitting in to regular school, and as his birthday got closer, his difficulties seemed to be getting greater. He had trouble sleeping. His mother would cuddle him at night and talk to him about his fears—he had terrific fears about going to sleep. And we had a child psychologist see him, because we couldn't understand why he had these fears.

Well, over the next several months he got better, and he seemed to be coming out of his depression. He started to say he wanted to have a party—his belated birthday party—but he didn't want it to be called a birthday party. He wanted it to be called a Happy Spring party. So we planned it, and he wanted to just have three friends. He had a friend named Ben, a little girlfriend named Jamie, and he had a boy named Cam that had always wanted to be friends with him, but Brian didn't really spend much time with them. It was kind of like he was trying to finish up unfinished business.

Now during the two weeks before the party, Brian did lots of unusual things. He got Kathryn's Mother's Day card in advance and a present. Mother's Day was two weeks away. And then he also got my Father's Day present, even though that was months away. He got a trophy he picked out that said World's Greatest Dad, and he begged Kathryn to get it, but she said, "It's a couple months away. We don't have to do that yet." He wrote letters to his grandparents—all the things that he'd been planning to do and hadn't done, and his spirits seemed to be getting much better. So it was a couple of days before his party, and Kathryn came home and Brian had a little red wagon. He was pulling a red wagon down the driveway, and he had his camping gear on there and his toys and teddy bears. Kathryn said, "Brian, what are you doing?" And Brian said, "I'm ready to go on my trip." And Kathryn said, "Well, you can't go away, because we have your birthday party coming up," and he said, "All right."

And then the next morning was the morning of his birthday party. So he woke up, and he wrote letters to some of his friends and put a sign on his door. We didn't realize it till later. The sign said: "On a trip. Don't worry about me." And then the kids came for the party, and they had a great little party. He didn't want any gifts, but his little girlfriend gave him a kiss, and his friend Ben wrote a song for him. And then it was time for them to leave and for Brian to play Little League. He'd just joined this team. He wasn't very good. He was the littlest kid on the team. I took him, and Kathryn was going to join us a little bit later, and we got to the end of the driveway, and Brian said, "I've got these letters to mail on the way." And I looked at them, and I said, "Brian, these letters don't have any stamps on them. You know they won't get mailed," and Brian said, "But Dad, you don't understand. They will get there." He was very hardheaded, so I didn't argue with him, and we put the letters into the mailbox. And this was on Saturday. And then we went to the baseball field.

When Brian got there, he was so brave. He had always been afraid of the ball and kind of tried to shrink away from ground balls and stuff like that. But he was fearless. He was charging after the ground balls, and he was really just having the best time. He had said he wanted to score a run more than anything. So I was sitting in the stands, and it was his first time up at bat. He got walked to first base. The next little boy hit a triple, and Brian ran around the bases, crossed home plate. This was his second game, and the last time he got stranded at third base and didn't make it home. So this time he tore around the bases, crossed home plate, and the fans gave him a big applause. And he looked up at the stands and our eyes met, and he was the happiest little boy you ever saw. He gave me a high five and went into the dugout.

And then he collapsed. And the coach brought him out—his limp body out—and I looked at him, and he was blue. And I'm an anesthesiologist, and that's what I do is resuscitate people, and I resuscitated him. But something inside told me he wasn't coming back. The ambulance came, which was right across the street, and we went to the hospital with him. They tried to resuscitate him, and he wouldn't come back.

After he died, I went to the ball field to get my car, and it was the most beautiful spring day I have ever seen. The next day was Mother's Day. The honeysuckle was out, which for that early in the year is very unusual, and there was another Little League game playing and barbecues going on with square dancing in the picnic shelters around the field. And I was standing in the field looking at the other kids playing, and I smelled the honeysuckle, and the clouds were beautiful—crisp, blue sky—and I smelled the barbecue. I reached up to wipe a tear from my eye, and I had vomit—the smell of vomit from Brian when I tried to resuscitate him. When you shock somebody, they often vomit, because their muscles tense up. And as I wiped my eye, the smell of the vomit combined with the smell of the honeysuckle and the barbecue, and then all of a sudden everything got very clear. I've since heard other people describe this kind of great moment—that I could see everything clearer than I'd ever seen. The colors were clearer and brighter, and the smells were stronger, and I had the sense that everything was okay. I was at peace. And that if I could bring Brian back, it would be for me, not for him—that he had finished. He had finished his job here, and the unfinished business was just mine.

June 3, 2005

KATHERINE MEERS, 16,
interviews her father, SAM MEERS, 45

RECORDED IN NEW YORK CITY

Katherine Meers: What's your first memory of Mom?

Sam Meers: I saw her come into my freshman English class wearing green corduroys and a brown sweater. She was delivering notes to the teacher. And I thought, "Wow, there's a really cute girl." I really didn't get to know her very well until my junior year when she came to visit me at Dairy Queen, where I was working. But we still didn't date. She ended up dating my best friend in high school. And then one morning in late January of 1978 we were talking—you know, we had lockers next to each other—and I remember saying to her, "If David doesn't take you to see *Oh, God!* with John Denver and George Burns, then I'll take you." And she said, "Sam Meers, if you want to take me to a movie, you should ask me." So I did. And that shortly ended David's and my friendship.

Katherine: But it was worth it.

Sam: You're living proof. You know, one of the hard things about your mom dying was that I never, ever fell out of love with her. And that kind of changes how I look at my relationship with Julie, my wife now, because I didn't go through a divorce or anything like that. That love is still there, and it always will be. It's just a different kind of love. And it's a memory that I cherish greatly.

You know, she and your brother, Michael, were both diagnosed with cancer within thirty days of each other. And actually it was interesting. Michael was diagnosed with a brain tumor in early October, and then she was diagnosed with breast cancer in early November.

Katherine: That's when I was starting first grade.

Sam: Right. Both of them went through chemo together. Michael died in April 1997, and she died in August of 1998. But you know, in both cases I had plenty of time personally, as you did, too, to say good-bye and to really understand what was going to happen. And I think that gives us a huge advantage over people that lose family members where there was no opportunity to say good-bye. It helps you reconcile what happened and what's going to happen.

Katherine: I would be in the kitchen playing a game or something, or getting food, and I just remember thinking to myself, "I shouldn't be having fun, you know, knowing that half of my family is going to be dead in a short amount of time."

Sam: Your mom had always told me, from the moment she was diagnosed, that the breast cancer would probably kill her. Of course I didn't believe that. But after Michael died, you know, what she wanted to do was be with Michael.

Katherine: And she kind of lost the will to—

Sam: She lost the will to live. And, you know, she and I had more than one conversation about you and I being okay, and she and Michael being okay. It's just that we wouldn't be together.

Katherine: Yeah. That's difficult for me, because I wanted her to stay. But she didn't want to stay.

Sam: Well, she knew you'd be okay, you know? She knew you well enough to know that in the eight or nine years that you had been here, that you were well grounded and mature and smart.

Katherine: I know for me, I really don't like to remember Mom at the end of her life. I always imagine her with those gold earrings that I got her for Valentine's Day and that red-and-white-striped shirt. That's kind of the image that's always in my mind.

Sam: I try really hard not to remember the last three or four months. It's hard not to think about that, because once somebody's dying from cancer, it's a fairly memorable experience. But the thing I do remember about the night she died—you know, she died maybe a little after midnight. And I remember the chimes on the deck that blew.

Katherine: Michael's chimes.

Sam: Yeah, about ten minutes after she died. And that was on a very still night in August.

Katherine: I remember hospice came in, and they had set up everything in the living room. And I was on the couch, and I was just kind of laying there. And I just remember thinking to myself, "You know, it's going to happen, and there's nothing you can do about it. And I'm ready." And I just remember opening the blinds on my left and kind of being like, "Come on in. You can take her. It's okay. We're ready." And not long after that, I fell asleep on the couch, and you picked me up and carried me to my room. And that was it. In the next two minutes she was gone.

Sam: One of the interesting things the hospice people told me before she died was that typically people won't die while you're in the room. So I carried you to bed. And so she waited until both of us were out of the room before she died.

Katherine: She just knew.

Sam: Mmm-hmm. She was waiting. She was tired. We were tired. We left the room, and she died.

Katherine: How are you different?

Sam: I don't think anyone can go through those kinds of experiences and not be changed by them. You get an appreciation for life that strengthens you. And if it doesn't strengthen you, it weakens you. Really, you come to that fork in the road, and it's either A or B. Either you move through it and come out on the other side stronger, or you don't move through it.

Katherine: That's what I said when Michael had all of his surgery and Mom was feeling down. I was like, "We're in the mud puddle, but we'll get out."

Sam: It's interesting. I mean, many times your mom and I talked about whether or not we were actually sane, because at certain points Michael was on twenty-seven different medications a day and he had 24/7 care. And then it would just get progressively worse. I don't think most people realize the mental and physical capacity that they have until you're put in that situation. I referred to it as "Being on the front lines of a battle." You're just there. And from October of 1995 through August of 1998, it was a three-year battle. I remember waking up the morning after Michael died, and there was just nothing to do. And then, after your mom died, it was like there was really nothing to do.

Katherine: Do you think there's something that you know about Mom that no one else knows?

Sam: I know she was insecure about her abilities. You know she was incredibly smart. She was valedictorian of her high school class. She was a CPA. But she was somewhat insecure when it came to her abilities. I think she overcame that when Michael got sick. She really took charge of that situation. She pinned a doctor against the wall one time at Children's Mercy. I'd forgotten about that. But you know, she just grabbed him by the lapels. And he actually asked the nurse to call Security to get your mom off of him. It was just one of those situations when you have someone in your family that's in the hospital, you need to be an advocate for them. And she was absolutely an advocate for Michael. And she wasn't getting the answer she wanted. And so this feisty brunette pushes this doctor up against the wall and grabs him by the lapels. It was pretty intense there for a little bit. It's kind of funny, actually, as you look back on it now.

Katherine *(laughing)*: Well, I guess one of the reasons that I ask that is when I started high school, I started thinking that I only knew Mom as Mom, but not really as a person or as a wife or a daughter or a friend or anyone else. So when Julie was in the basement one day, she said that she found this box of stuff from Mom. And I went down and looked at it, and there were all of these journals from when she was in high school. And I'm reading them now. And I'm reading them as I go through high school. So I'm in her junior year, because I'm in my junior year. And it's interesting to see what she was talking about and how it relates to me

Sam: Somewhere in that box is also a sealed letter to you.

Katherine: I saw it, too. A sealed letter to me. I was planning to open it when I graduated high school. I thought I'd wait until a special moment. I just didn't know when.

Sam: What do you think about being born on your mom's birthday?

Katherine: I think it's pretty cool. When I was little I didn't really like it, because I had to share a birthday with someone. (*Crying.*) It was kind of annoying. But now I really like it. It was really difficult the first year after she died, because she wasn't there. It was the first time that I only had my birthday, my own birthday all to myself. And that was sad. But now it's just a way to remember and celebrate her. How old would she be?

Sam: She would be forty-six this November 16. I think she would be very proud of you. I think she would look at you and say that you've turned out to be everything she thought you would turn out to be.

Katherine: That's the way I'd like it to be.

Sam: She'd be very, very, very happy.

October 9, 2005

HISTORY

and

STRUGGLE

StoryCorps was created to give participants a powerful and at times transformative experience in the booth. Out of these interviews emerge both the story excerpts that we share with the nation and the archive housed at the Library of Congress.

These interviews will eventually grow into an oral history of America, painting a picture of who we were and how we lived in the twentieth and twenty-first centuries. History is often told from a top-down perspective—focused on the experiences of politicians and the privileged. StoryCorps will instead create a bottom-up history of our country through the stories and voices of everyday Americans. For future listeners these interviews will illustrate who we were, what we cared about, and how we lived our day-to-day lives.

What follows is a series of personal stories that shine a light on just a few of the touchstone historic events of our time: the Depression, World War II, the civil rights era, Vietnam, and the age of AIDS. It is in no way a complete record of all the significant events of the twentieth and twenty-first centuries but, rather, a collection of on-the-ground snapshots of a handful of milestones that have helped shape our recent history.

VIRGINIA HILL FAIRBROTHER, 81,
interviewed by her daughter
LAUREL KAAE, 50

RECORDED IN BISMARCK, NORTH DAKOTA

Virginia Hill Fairbrother: I was born in 1924, so I started
school in 1930. The Depression was not evident the first
couple years. By the time I was in third grade, it was. We
had a brother and sister in school who only had one pair
of overshoes, and that was a nasty winter. One of the kids
came to school wearing the overshoes one day and got the
work. The next day the next kid came and did the same thing.
They only got half as much school as they should have, but
they passed.

My big memory was in 1936, which was our coldest year.
It was 60 degrees below in Parshall, North Dakota, that winter. That's the year that I consider my *odoriferous* year. I don't
know if there's a word like *odoriferous*, but it sure fits the year.
I was in sixth grade. Everybody came in with their mittens. I
don't know if anyone now realizes how mittens smell when
they're wet with snow, but we'd all come in and put our mittens on the radiators to dry—and you already had a very different odor.

The teacher kept us in alphabetical order, so the fellow
ahead of me was Billy Bernt. Billy Bernt's father was a First
World War veteran. He had been wounded. He didn't have any
money. They were a nice family—very clean. But Billy only

had two sets of clothes. At night in the wintertime he ran a trap line, and every so often he got skunks. He didn't need to tell us the next day that he'd gotten a skunk. We knew it. He sat ahead of me.

On either side of me there were a brother and sister who were farmer's children. They walked a mile to school in this weather. They again didn't have any money. Their mother made bread, and she put lard on the bread, and either wild garlic or wild onion. When they came, they had their lunch pails. You weren't aware of it then, but about an hour after they had eaten it, you knew somebody had eaten garlic or onions.

In the kitty-corner in back of me was a girl who got up at five o'clock every morning and went to our doctor's office with her mother and washed everything with disinfectant. You could smell that. I have no idea what I smelled like.

A lot of people at that time still didn't have bathrooms inside, so they didn't wash as much as they should have or could have. All of the little girls in those days, if you had a birthday, you got a bottle of Blue Waltz perfume, which had kind of a vanilla odor. You got four ounces for ten cents. So every girl used perfume. The little boys used cough drops with a licorice odor. All of those things together made an odor that I still think of every so often. Once in a while I smell some of that stuff, and I go back to sixth grade.

We had a wonderful teacher who never said a word about the smell. We had to spend five minutes of the recess time outside, and then we could come in because it was so cold. While we were out, she raised all of the windows, and when we got in, it was colder than you could believe, but there was no odor for a little while. She must have been an angel.

My dad, Homer Hill, gave me my feeling of self-worth. He gave me a feeling of history and where I belong. He said the most important thing for anyone is their own name—so you learn somebody's name. You don't call them "Hey."

His dad died while being operated on the kitchen table when he was nine. Somehow or another my dad got a herding job when he was eleven years old. Each family in Harvey, North Dakota, had their own milk cow. In the summertime they sent these cows out into the hills.

One of the men who was responsible for several different herds saw him and asked him what he did besides herding. He said there wasn't much to do. This man gave him a book of Shakespeare and a book of poetry. My dad knew more Shakespeare and more poetry, and it was because of this man. It got to be November, about the time that kids went to school in those days. This fellow came through, and he saw my dad out in the hills again and he said, "Homer, why aren't you in school?" My dad answered, "Nobody came to get the cattle." In three hours there were people there to get the cattle. The man told him to go into Harvey, get a haircut, and start school the next day. Dad always said that without the interest from this man, he would have been another lost little boy without an education on the prairie.

My dad was a registered pharmacist. He had a drugstore

in town for forty-four years. Every noon when Dad had eaten, we always went out and walked around our yard and picked weeds and commented on the flowers. One day this old car drove up in front of the house, and a man got out and called Dad by name. Dad went over there, and the man said, "Someone in town told me that you might help feed my family."

He was a young fellow who had just graduated from the University of Minnesota. This man had a wife and two sons in this car. He was an engineer, and he said if he could get to Fort Peck by the next day, he would have a job. Dad took them into the restaurant and had them fed. He had a friend of his who was a Ford dealer fill the car with gas and put on a spare tire. He gave this man a sackful of food that wasn't perishable and five dollars.

Twenty-five years later I happened to be in my folks' home one night. My brother, who was a pharmacist, was in the drugstore. He called and said, "Somebody just came in and asked to talk to Mr. Hill." This man was looking for Dad, so he sent him up to our house. He came in, and he had two tall young men with him. He said to Dad, "You don't know me, do you, Mr. Hill? I'm the fellow that had to get to Fort Peck."

On that day all those years ago, the young man had insisted on giving Dad a watch that he had gotten from his father for graduation. Dad looked at Mother and said, "Florence—the watch." My mother went and got it from where it had been all of those years, except on Sundays when Dad wound it. He gave it back to the fellow. The man said, "You were supposed to use this." Dad said, "I did. Every Sunday I wound it."

This man never expected to see his watch again. He just wanted his kids to see my dad.

July 14, 2005

MANNY DIAZ JR., 81, interviewed by his friend BLANCA VÁSQUEZ, 56

RECORDED IN NEW YORK CITY

Manny Diaz Jr.: I was born September 19, 1922, and I came to New York from Puerto Rico in 1927. And when we came from Puerto Rico, Puerto Ricans did not exist. We used to call ourselves Spaniards because nobody knew what Puerto Ricans were in those days. There were no more than ten thousand or eleven thousand of us living in New York City—mostly in East Harlem or on the Lower East Side of Manhattan.

We lived at 37 West 114th Street in a five-story tenement house. That building had Italian families, one black family, Jewish families—you name it. It was like a microcosm of the United Nations. This was during the Depression, the poor days. There was no surplus food program in those days, but the Army used to send in trucks now and then and dump food on the street. People would come and pick up apples or corn. But the day that we all looked forward to was the day when the trucks dumped grapes. "*Oye! Oye!* The grapes are here! The grapes are here!" Everybody used to run with a baby carriage, with pushcarts, with pillowcases to pick up the grapes that were dumped by the U.S. Army trucks, and then we would bring those grapes home.

We would put the grapes in the bathtub, crush them, and

then go to Woolworth's, where you would pick up the burlap bag to cover the grapes, the yeast, the sugar, the bottles, the corks, and even the little gadget where you put the cork into the bottle. This was Prohibition, but Woolworth's will sell you anything that you needed to brew your stuff. And then you wonder what happens when people want to take a bath? Well, in this building was a kind of a mutual assistance society. Everybody helped everybody else, so if your bathtub is incapacitated for whatever reason, you just go to your neighbor and say, "Can I use your bathtub?"

We would sell a quart of wine for twenty-five cents, and we would give wine to our neighbors. There was an Italian seaman on the third floor who used to go away for a month or so. When he came back, instead of buying pork chops for his family, he would buy a whole pig. And we'd go up to the rooftop and roast that pig. Everybody from that building ate the pig from the Italian guy and drank the wine from the Diaz family. And that's how you survived through the Depression. "Everybody's poor and nobody feels poor." That's an old axiom.

I went to Stuyvesant High School, but I got to tell you how I got in there. Stuyvesant High School is one of the elite schools in the city of New York, and they usually rank first or second or third in national exams. I graduated from junior high, and in those days there were no guidance counselors, so I got placed at the Haaren High School for aviation trade, and I loved it because all we did was play with model airplanes. I was at Haaren about a week when my mother was told this was the worst school in the city of New York, and without missing a beat, she said, "Well, what is the best school in the city of New York?" The answer came back that Stuyvesant was the best school in the city of New York.

So would you believe, next Monday morning my mother had me in the office of the principal of Stuyvesant High School, Mr. Wilson? As we walked in, Mr. Wilson asked, "What can we do for you?" and she says, "I want my son in the best school of the city of New York." "Oh, Mrs. Diaz, we're into the term. It's very difficult to—" "Mr. Wilson, I want my son in the best school of the city of New York." "Well, Mrs. Diaz, you see, we require an 86 average, and your son has only a 71 average, so I'm not sure we—" "Mr. Wilson, you do not understand. I want my son in the best school of the city of New York."

I guess Mr. Wilson was frustrated, so he gave me what many years later I realized was an aptitude test, which was maybe forty-five minutes long. My mother sat across the room wagging a finger at me like in effect saying, "You'd better do good or else!" I finally finished and turned in the papers to Mr. Wilson, and then as we left the office there, my mother turns around and says, "Mr. Wilson, do not forget: I want my son in the best school of the city of New York." What do you know? A week later we get a notice that I have been transferred to Stuyvesant High School. I wonder whether that aptitude test is what opened the door for me or whether Mr. Wilson was just too afraid that my mother might come back. I did well at Stuyvesant. I ended up with a 92 average.

Those are my experiences in East Harlem—the life and times of Manny Diaz.

February 25, 2004

DEBRA A. FISHER, 45, interviewed by facilitator KAREN DIMATTIA, 30

RECORDED IN NEW YORK CITY

Debra A. Fisher: I learned about the Holocaust sort of in a backdoor way. My earliest memory was of my father buying two of everything. It didn't matter if it was roller skates for me or a basketball for my brother. It didn't matter if it was candy and I just wanted one; it was always two—just in case. Just in case it's cold and you need another blanket, just in case you lose that basketball and you don't want to wait, you don't have to wait.

He never waited on line. I remember that. We never, never waited on line. I remember we went to Disney World, and my father didn't make a reservation for dinner. We couldn't get in anywhere. We had to wait two or three hours, and my father was beside himself trying to find a place for us to eat. For us to be hungry was very, very bad. I remember him walking over to the maitre d', looking down at the desk at the reservation book, reading it upside down, and saying, "We are the Weinbergs, seven o'clock," and they sat us. And my mother, who was born in this country, was mortified, and I remember her saying to my father, "What are we going to do if the Weinbergs come, Oscar?" and he said, "We are going to eat fast." We never waited, not in a movie line—nothing. Because the line was for people to die, and that was how he framed his life.

The image of Auschwitz that I had from my dad was what I refer to as "Robin Hood and His Merry Men" or the "Our Gang" series—a bunch of boys running around. The Nazis were evil, and we always outsmarted them. There was a table full of bread. They said, "Don't touch or we'll kill you." They turned their backs; we boys grabbed some, we put it in our pajamas. It was a very upbeat Auschwitz.

I had no idea that his Auschwitz was the same as Elie Wiesel's Auschwitz in *Night*. I remember at about fourteen I read the book, and I went to my father and I said, "Dad, this man, he was in Auschwitz. This is a very, very horrible place and a horribly sad story and his father died, just like your father. Auschwitz was terrible." And he said, "Our Auschwitz was different. There were two Auschwitzes. There was that Auschwitz, and then there was our Auschwitz, where it wasn't like that." So I believed him. I grew up thinking there were two Auschwitzes. He won against the Nazis—him and his band of boys. He outsmarted them. I asked him, but he really didn't want to talk about it. He really, really didn't. He worked damn hard at it.

Unfortunately, my father contracted hepatitis and got very sick. He was in the hospital and more and more debilitated. At one point they changed my father's medication, and he was sort of lucid. I brought a pad and a pen and said, "Dad, I need to ask you some questions about Auschwitz. I don't want to hurt you, but I need to have these questions answered." He was really upset. "All of your childhood you keep asking me questions, and I keep answering them, and it's never enough!" And he became very, very angry. He said, "It's like since you were a little girl, you've been banging on this door in a room that I'm in all by myself. You keep saying, 'Daddy, let me in the room! Let me in the room!' And I keep saying, 'Go away! You cannot come in here!' And you keep banging on the door, and I keep telling you to go away. And here you are again banging on that door!" And his voice was raised. He turned beet red, and he was so agitated, and he said to me, "Debbie, if I open this door and I let you in this room, you will never be able to leave this room. You'll be in this room forever. It will be a nightmare you cannot get rid of. You will wake up to it, and you will go to sleep with it. That's what's in this room, and I do not want to open that door for you."

I said, "But, Dad, I need for you to." And he just was so angry that he kicked the covers off of his legs—almost violently, like punching at the air—and said, "Fine. The door is open. Now you can come in. Come in. You happy?" And he was yelling at me, and I said, "Dad, I just need to know," and he said, "What is it you need to know?"

I proceeded to ask my questions. And he proceeded to answer.

The images that he painted for me in that room, what happened to him and his brothers and others around him, they were so horrific. I felt a part of me die. And slowly I realized that he was right: Once you enter that room, you cannot leave. I am in that room when I sleep and when I wake. It's always with me.

September 9, 2004

JOSEPH L. ROBERTSON, 87, interviewed
by his son-in-law, JOHN H. FISH JR., 61

RECORDED IN COLUMBUS, OHIO

John H. Fish Jr.: Over the years you've mentioned how you enlisted in the Army before World War II as a young man— not quite eligible, not quite old enough.

Joseph L. Robertson: I went to Fort Bragg, North Carolina, to visit my brother who was in the service. His CO asked me, "Why don't you join the Army?" And I said, "I'm not old enough. I'm only sixteen." He said, "I heard you—you're seventeen. It's what's you have to be." I said, "I'm sixteen." He said, "That's right. I heard you. You're seventeen." So, next day, I was in military service.

Four years after I enlisted, war broke out, and we were mobilized the next day. I was with the Thirtieth Reconnaissance Troop, Thirtieth Infantry Division. I was the only one who wasn't killed, captured, or wounded. We were scheduled to land on D-day. But the Twenty-ninth Infantry Division ahead of us had a terrible time landing, and we didn't make it in. We went back out into the ocean and spent the night behind the battleship *Texas* because we were in a little landing craft with no weapons other than one machine gun.

John: Once you got on the beach the day after D-day, what happened?

Joseph: Well, the Germans were good at firing on vehicles.

They knew exactly where your fuel tank was, so they hit the fuel tank. Our armored car blew up, killing the lieutenant, the gunner, and the radio operator immediately. It was on fire. The driver was pinned in and could not get out, so all he could do was scream for somebody. "Please! Shoot me!" Three people shot him. We had to.

John: And one of the stories that you talk about is the young German soldiers from the Hitler Youth.

Joseph: Well, the platoon sergeant from the infantry had killed so many of these kids that he was losing it; he was crying like a baby himself. One of his friends came up and took over his machine gun, a .30 caliber. They kept coming straight; they didn't veer to the left or the right. Although everyone in front of them was going down dead, they kept coming, and he kept shooting them. He left, and one of his friends came up and took his place.

The German kids were Hitler Youth, all dressed in their black SS uniforms. They were aged from twelve to fourteen, and they didn't know how to stop. One of them was coming out of the woods. I hid behind a big tree that was knocked down. I could see these Germans in the woods across this big field, and I saw this young kid crawling up a ditch, straight toward my tree. So I let him crawl. I didn't fire at him, but when he got up within three or four feet of me, I screamed at him to surrender. We all used the same word, *Kamerad,* and instead of surrendering, he started to pull his gun toward me, which was instant death for him.

This young man—he was a blond, blue eyes, fair-skinned,

so handsome. He was like a little angel, but I still had to shoot him. And it didn't bother me the first night because I was so tired, I went to sleep. But the second night I woke up crying, because that kid was there. And to this day I wake up many nights crying over this kid. I still see him in my dreams. And I don't know how to get him off my mind.

July 17, 2005

Joseph L. Robertson (l.) and
John H. Fish Jr. (r.)

. . . .

MARIE DESANTIS, 78, interviewed by her
daughter, MARY-LU HAYES, 51, and her
grandson, MARK HAYES, 22

RECORDED IN NEW YORK CITY

Marie DeSantis: My brother Joe was the last one of his
buddies to go into the service during the Second World War.
When he was going for his physical, my mother said, "I don't
want to wish anything on you, but oh I hope they find something wrong with you so you don't have to go." And my brother
Joe, he says, "Mama, if they find something wrong with me and
I don't go, I'm jumping over the bridge on the way home. I
have to go. Everybody's there."

They used to come and bring you the telegrams. One night
here comes the man with a telegram. I read the telegram; it
says, "We regret to inform you that your son Joseph is missing in action." I was drying the spoons and forks. My family
was at church, two blocks away. I ran up to the church to tell
them what happened. So I said, "Hurry up. Come home,
come home. Joey's missing in action." And they all came
home. My sister, instead of getting in the car and driving
home, ran home alongside the car. It was the worst news you
could get. Believe me, from the bottom of my heart. It
was terrible.

We went home, and, of course, every neighbor came in the
house; it was awful. Mama was a very funny person. She says,
"Well, it's getting closer to Christmas. We don't know where

he is, so we can't have a Christmas tree, because Joey will not be here to trim it. We can't celebrate it."

So, of course, we abided by her wishes. On Christmas Eve we get a letter, and the letter says, "I'm in a hospital. By now you must be putting up the Christmas tree, and I want you to know that I'm all right. I'll come home soon, and I'll be all right. And, Mama, don't worry about me." I want to cry now talking about it.

So she says, "Oh my God! Oh my God! We didn't get the Christmas tree! And look what happened: He's telling us to decorate the Christmas tree." And my brother John says, "Ma, don't worry about it. Last night when I came from work, I bought a Christmas tree, and I put it under the porch. I thought maybe you would change your mind and we could have our Christmas tree."

And we did.

June 9, 2005

．　．　．　．　．　．　．　．　．　．　．

SAM HARMON, 75, interviewed by his grandson EZRA AWUMEY, 12

RECORDED IN WASHINGTON, D.C.

Sam Harmon: I was born in the year that the stock market crashed, in 1929. My first recollection is in 1932. A lot of poor people were around, a lot of what we called "hobos" moving around the country, train to train. I remember in Detroit a homeless hungry man would show up at our kitchen door and knock and ask if my mother had any leftover food that she could give him. We never refused. We always agreed to do so and were happy to. That was always a good memory that I had in those days—how generous people were towards those who did not have.

I joined the Navy at fifteen. The reason I lied about my age was because I was patriotic and wanted to fly a plane. When I was a boy, I hung around airports, washing airplanes. When I was fourteen, somebody said, "Hey, kid. Would you like to make a parachute jump?" And I did. So I was billed as the youngest parachutist in the world. Then they taught me how to fly, and I studied meteorology and radio communications— all in preparation to be drafted into the Army, assigned to the Air Force, transferred to Tuskegee, where I'd become a fighter pilot. That was my dream.

I didn't have a choice of which branch of service I went to. They assigned me to the Navy. During all of World War II, black sailors in the Navy had only one job: to act as servants to the white officers—clean their beds, wash their clothes, cook them food, serve them. Just purely servants. I resisted. I said, "You can't draft me to fight for the country and then discriminate." So I spent the first few months of my Navy career in the brig. One day I found myself hallucinating. I was in isolation, sitting on this bench, flying the bench as though it was an airplane, and I was shooting down zeroes off the wall, and I realized that the hallucination was worse for me than it was for the Navy. So I decided to capitulate and went to work in the kitchen.

After three weeks they abruptly transferred me to a job that no other black guy in the Navy had ever been considered for: training as an electronic technician. That came about because the personnel man looked at my IQ scores and said, "It's a shame that you have to work in the kitchen." It turned out he simply went into the files and classified me as a Caucasian, and nobody knew the difference or cared.

Ezra Awumey: What was the saddest moment in your life?

Sam: Early in the Navy I was stationed in Norfolk, Virginia. One day my shipmates and I decided to come to Washington to visit the capital, this great center of democracy. I drove the car; I didn't drink at the time, so I would be the designated driver. While they were at the bars, I decided to sightsee. I walked around the monuments all day. I was just tired out. And I decided that I would go to a movie, rest, and then pick them up later.

It was right there on Pennsylvania Avenue—it was First Street, I think. There was a movie house there, and I went up to buy a ticket. There was a glass with the ticket seller behind it, and off of the glass reflected the Capitol dome. And I just thought to myself, "What a great way to end the day—drinking in all of this democracy." I called for the ticket. She was reading. She punched the machine. I reached my hand to get the ticket and lay down the money. She pulled it back. And she said, "You can't come in here." She saw my black hand and refused to sell me a ticket. The Capitol dome was superimposed on her angry face—angered that I would have the temerity to ask to buy a ticket. And I just walked the streets crying all night, betrayed that my country could force me to fight a war but say, "You're not a good enough citizen to come to a movie."

You know, it's emotional. My vocabulary is more of a scientific one, so I can't answer your question as fluently as I'd like. Even though it took me a while to remember, that's the most painful recollection of anything that's ever happened to me. The saddest moment—without any exception.

May 19, 2005

THERESA BURROUGHS, 76, interviewed by her daughter, TONI LOVE, 36

RECORDED IN TUSCALOOSA, ALABAMA

Theresa Burroughs: I was born in Greensboro, which is about forty-something miles south of Tuscaloosa, where we are now. I was born and reared there. And I attended school there. And when I was growing up, you would call this the segregated South. As a child I did not know the difference, because really we didn't even have to deal with white people because we didn't come in contact with them. There were black schools, black churches, and black civic organizations.

But every once in a while segregation will smack you in the face. I was about ten years old, and this group of five or six of us were sitting on the side of the road on a little bank, and this white man came by in a truck. He was a collector, and he was looking for some people who owed this company he worked for. He asked if we knew where those people lived. I said, "Yes, I know."

So he jumps out of the truck, and he comes over to me— I'm ten years old now. He sticks his finger in my face and he said, "Don't you ever say 'yes' to a white person! Don't you ever do that!" He says to me, "Whenever you speak to a white person, you say 'yes, sir' or 'no, sir,' 'yes, ma'am' and 'no, ma'am.'" Imagine a big white man telling you this and you're ten years old! I started running, and I ran home to my mother. She saw me coming, and she just opened her arms. I just fell up in her arms, and I was crying because no one had ever spoken to me in that tone before, and it hurt me so bad. She didn't say anything. She just held me real close and said, "Listen," she said, "I have some cake and I baked some cookies." I said, "Oh, you have?" But it stayed with me the rest of my life. I can see it now just as it happened yesterday.

I started going to town, and I noticed that if we were to meet white people on the street, the blacks would have to step off the sidewalk and let the white people walk on the sidewalk. Even though you've just polished your shoes and it's raining, you're going to have to step off. And I would say, "There's something wrong with this." And what really got my goat is when I became eligible to vote and they would not let me vote because I was black.

I was always wanting to vote. I'm a history buff. I started reading history books when I was five or six years old. And they promised in the history book that all men are created equally. We're endowed by our creator with certain inalienable rights like liberty and the pursuit of happiness. And yet here I am of age, and I could not vote. Something was wrong.

The first and third Mondays of the month were voter registration days. You could only go those two days. I would go every time they opened the doors. I was standing there along with a minister named Reverend J. J. Simmons. He pastored one of the largest churches in Hale County. We would go and stand there all day long. The white men in the courthouse had tables, and they would sit there and play dominoes. I didn't even know how to play dominoes, but I learned by looking at them. They would not let us register to vote. I went for two years. I just kept going.

One Monday, Reverend Simmons and I had about five other people with us. We were standing along the wall of the courthouse. The white men were playing dominoes. They were having a good time, and we're standing, wanting to vote. They wouldn't even let us lean. "Get off that wall! Don't lean against that wall!" This was what they were saying to us. And we would have to stand there with our arms folded, standing just like prisoners, trying to register to vote.

This man—I never will forget his name—Mr. Cocke. He was chair of the Board of Registrars, and he would ask you silly questions like "How many black jelly beans in this jar? How many red ones?" He would hold up a jar of jelly beans. Oh, my goodness, silly questions like that. One day I told him, "You don't know how many jelly beans there are in there." He told me to shut my black mouth. Reverend Simmons just held my hand. He just reached out and took my hand.

And so the next Monday when we were supposed to go, I told him that I was not going back. "I can't, because I'm not going to be embarrassed like that anymore." He said, "Oh, you're going back. You want to vote, don't you?" I said, "Yes." He said, "We're going to go until the building falls down. We're going to be there every time they open that door. We're going to be there." He said, "Now in the morning I'll be by to pick you up. You're going." And that is the day that Mr. Cocke asked me to recite part of the preamble to the Constitution. I recited it. I don't really think he knew it, but he gave me my slip that I was a registered voter. Reverend Simmons got his slip that same day. The two of us. Mr. Cocke said, "You're going to pass today because we are tired of looking at your black faces."

We did vote in the next election. But what you must know is that even after we passed, we still had to pay a poll tax. We had to pay one dollar and fifty cents before we could get our qualifications. But we went out on our own, we stood on our own, and we passed on our own. It was just a coming of time, as the Bible says. "In the fullness of time, all things come to pass." And it was just time.

November 21, 2005

Retired sanitation worker TAYLOR ROGERS, 79, speaks with his wife, BESSIE ROGERS

RECORDED IN MEMPHIS, TENNESSEE

Taylor Rogers: Back in 1968, sanitation workers decided we were tired and weren't going to take no more. I was trying to raise eight kids. We had troubled working conditions, low salary. It was awful. You go deep back in these backyards, dump the garbage out of these fifty-gallon drums into these tubs, put that tub on your head or on your shoulder, bring it out to the truck, dump it, and move on to the next house. Most of those tubs had holes in them, and garbage would leak all over you.

At lunchtime we had to stand beside the truck and eat lunch. We didn't have no place to wash our hands or nothing. We just had to stop and eat wherever we could. By the time you got home in the evening, you had to pull off all those dirty clothes where maggots had fell all on you. Our day was awful every day. But we had a family to raise and to take care of, and that's what we did.

Bessie Rogers: If it was raining, they said they would let them work a half a day if they wanted to, but they would dock them for the rest of the day. Most of the time they'd just stay up there and work in the rain. In the sleet, in snow, they'd still have to work there, regardless. They didn't have no kind of benefits at all. It was just terrible.

Taylor: One of the main things that really upset us all real good was that two of the workers got in their compactors to get out of the rain one rainy day, and they tripped some kind of lever that threw that thing up on them and crushed them to death. The family didn't get compensation. So we said, "This is it." We just got tired. We tried to organize to have a union. We decided we weren't going to work anymore. We were going to stand up and be men. That's what we did. We told the mayor, Henry Loeb: "I am a man."

Before we went on strike, I sat down and talked to the family. I had three boys and five girls. The boys said, "Daddy, we'll help you do anything you need to be done," and my girls said, "Daddy, we'll do what we can," and we were all in agreement not to go back and give in.

We marched sixty-five days, trying to get Loeb to understand our needs and our frustration. All we wanted was some decencies and some dignity. If you've bent your back, people will ride your back. But if you stand up straight, people can't ride your back. So that's what we did—we just stood up straight and said, "I am a man!"

Bessie: We had a whole lot of help. All the churches— there was a lot of white people. They came and helped, too. They were giving money, bringing food to the union hall. We had to pay our rent. Our bills still was going on.

We marched and we marched and we marched. We got sprayed. My children got sprayed in the face. Then they called in Martin Luther King. He decided to come down and help the sanitation workers.

Taylor: He stopped everything, set everything aside, to

come to Memphis to see about the people on the bottom of the ladder: the sanitation workers. The day before that march, that's the day he was assassinated.

Bessie: The night before he got killed, he was up at this big church, Mason Temple. I mean, there were so many people at that temple. It was storming and raining. Thousands of people were down there.

Taylor: It was wall to wall with people, and you could tell from the sound of his voice that he felt that something was going to happen.

Bessie: He preached, and he was crying. Tears were rolling down his cheek. I believe he kind of felt that something was going to happen to him.

Taylor: Preacher was crying. People were crying. Everybody was crying. And he put so much into that speech. You really could feel that something was going to happen to him.

Bessie: He really talked that night. I mean he really, *really* talked!

Taylor: He said, "I've been to the mountaintop. I've looked over, and I've seen the Promised Land. I may not get there with you, but we will get there." He said, "I'm not fearing any man. Mine eyes have seen the glory of the coming of the Lord." You could really tell he felt something was coming.

Bessie: The next day he was killed.

Taylor: It was kind of like you lost a part of your family. You just really can't describe it. To put aside everything to come here to see about people on the bottom of the ladder—I think I will always have that in my heart.

After his death we did have that march. You couldn't hear

a sound. You couldn't hear nothing but leather against pavement. Everybody had this deep sorrow. Everybody was just quiet and somber, but we wanted to be there because that's what he wanted done.

Bessie: They finally got the union, and they were treated fairly. They didn't have to go out and work in the rain, and they still got paid. Now the men don't even have to go in the backyard—we have to put the garbage out on the front. I tell those garbagemen when they come by, I say, "You all are blessed. Years ago my husband had the tub on the top of his head. Had to go way in the backyard and get the garbage." They're just blessed things have really worked out good for them. A man had to come in and give his life for them.

October 20, 2005

TOM GEERDES, 60, talks with his daughter
HANNAH CAMPBELL, 30

RECORDED IN MURRAY, KENTUCKY

Tom Geerdes: Even when I was in basic training, I felt a cloud over my head. I knew a lot of the guys that got drafted would go to Vietnam, and it was just kind of a darkness waiting. I really didn't plan on coming back. I just had that feeling.

When I got back, I didn't shave or cut my hair for probably a year. And in northwest Iowa that's not really acceptable behavior. Even some of my cousins and people I knew before I left didn't think too much of me after I got back.

So I took a long bicycle trip. I rode straight north up through Minnesota, nearly up to Winnipeg. And then I cut across, and I worked my way back up to Highway 1, in Canada, and rode all the way to the West Coast, to Vancouver, British Columbia. Took me about six weeks.

It helped a lot. But I actually didn't heal from Vietnam till I was in Murray, quite a number of years later. I had a janitorial business, and I was doing floors at Sears. They had a Vietnam movie on there. They had it on the TVs sitting all over the Sears. I was just kind of buffing floors and watching the movie on the TV.

And something just broke. And I cried. *(Crying.)* While I was finishing them floors, I just sobbed like a baby for a couple of hours. 'Cause it was several good friends I lost. And after that it was a process—a healing process. It was just a cleansing, I believe. Just too much devastation that I saw there, just too much hurt.

Hannah Campbell: I'm glad you came back.

Tom: Yeah, me too. Me too.

October 1, 2005

MARY CAPLAN, 60, interviewed by her friend EMILY COLLAZO, 41

RECORDED IN NEW YORK CITY

Mary Caplan: My brother Tom and I were very close. He was around a lot. He was godfather to my son Michael. Tom's partner— We didn't call them partners then. Tom's friend got what was then called "gay cancer." He called me and he told me that Bruce had it, and he said, "Do you know the survival rate?" I said no. He said, "It's zero." I said, "Tom, I'm a nurse. There's no such thing as zero survival rate even with the worst cancers. There can be a one percent survival rate." And he said, "With this, there's a zero." I remember frantically calling everyone and trying to get information. I can't even explain what it was like, because all of a sudden someone would say, "Don't ask that person. Don't let them know that you know someone that might have this." Tom was always deathly afraid of hospitals, but he went. He was with Bruce the whole time. He never left him.

Tom and I used to meet every Tuesday night for dinner. I was at school. It was winter. He had a stocking hat on, and he looked thinner, and it was cold. He sat down at the table. He had the most gorgeous eyes and eyelashes. I looked at his eyes and I said, "You're positive, aren't you?" He said, "Yeah." I said, "Are you frightened?" He said, "Yes." I said, "Tom, I'll stay with you all the way, and we'll do everything we can." He said, "I don't want to take any treatment, because there's really nothing there." We talked some more. I don't remember what we said.

I hugged him good-bye, and I took the elevator up to my class, and I sat down. And then all of a sudden it hit me. I was in class about five minutes, and I got up and left. I called my husband, Dick, and I was hysterical, crying. He said, "We'll do anything. We'll do anything." But there wasn't anything to do except be there. So I called Tom. There was some talk of something in Israel, something in Mexico. I couldn't rally the family around, because people were so afraid of the disease, and he hadn't come out to my mother. It was like the plague. I remember someone in my family being particularly afraid that a mosquito might bite Tom and then bite him, and then he'd have it. No one understood how it was spread. I called Tom, and I asked him what we could do. And he said, "I don't want to ever go to the hospital. I don't want to die in the hospital." And I said, "I promise you, you won't."

He got sick very quickly. I was going to bring him down to the shore for the summer, thinking that would be good for him. He always dressed really nicely. He wore blue oxford button-downs. So Friday I got to his apartment, and his blue shirt was on the floor, and he was just lying there like in a daze. I knew he was dehydrated because his eyes were sunken in. He said, "Don't panic." I said, "I'm not the panicking kind, Tom." Inside, I was panicked.

I had made a bed in the back of the car to take him down to the shore, and I went and I got his friend to help me get him out to the car, because I knew I couldn't get him out alone. He said, "I don't want to be in a hospital." I said, "Tom, I'm going to stop at a hospital just to get you something to make you comfortable, but I promise you I'm not going to leave you there. I'm going to bring you home." So I took him to New Jersey to the hospital.

It was the end of June 1986, and it was very hot. I went into the emergency room and said, "I need a stretcher. My brother's outside. He's sick, and he needs something for pain." And they said, "What's wrong with him?" And I said, "He has AIDS." They wouldn't come out and get him. He was out there, and it was 99 degrees. By this time he was starting to get comatose. I said, "If you don't come out and get him, I will pick him up and carry him in here and sit in the waiting room with him on my lap." That's what I was going to do. Then they scurried, and they all donned those suits—like in *E.T.*—and they came out.

I remember one nurse said to another, "Is he dead?" I just wanted to smash her. And they took him in, and I kept talking to him, and a doctor came down, this very nice woman doctor, and she said, "I can give him IVs and bring him back to consciousness, but he has meningitis and parasites, and he won't live long." I said to the doctor, "No, he doesn't want IVs. I'm a nurse, and I can take care of him at home. I think he needs some morphine, and he's going to become incontinent, and he's going to need some other things." I knew the things he would need and asked her for them. She was very good. She gave them to me.

I had to get a private ambulance to bring him home. The minute they moved him over to the ambulance everyone started running in with disinfectant and masks—as if he wasn't even a human being.

I brought him home, and the children were there. We all took care of him. I promised him I wouldn't leave the room, so they would bring me up sandwiches. I had to call my mother. I had to tell her he was gay, that he had AIDS, and he was dying—all at once. I sat with Tom, and I said, "You know, whenever you want to go, it's okay. I'll take care of Mom, and I'll take care of everything." And then he didn't go, and then I said, "Tom, I don't want you to think I'm rushing you, so you don't have to go."

I can't sing, and everyone knows I can't sing, and it was a big joke in the family. But I found myself, like I did with my children, singing lullabies. And I sang "Tura, Lura, Lura" to him one time, and I was so off-key, and when I finished, I kissed his forehead and I said, "I'm sorry. I know that wasn't very good." And then I went into the bathroom. And when I came back, he wasn't breathing. He died the moment I left.

Grief is when you get up the next day and you see the sun, and you say, "Will I ever think the sun is beautiful again?" And all of the normal parts of grieving. But the other parts that were so hard was I had this very educated woman come up to me and say, "Well, don't you think maybe God is telling us something by letting homosexuals die by this disease?" I wanted to slap her around. I wanted to physically harm her. And I just said, "No, I don't think so."

One day I went to a card shop, and there was a gay young man who worked there. I was buying a sympathy card—

another sympathy card—for one of Tom's friends. And this young man said something, and I said, "Well, I take care of my brother's friend. My brother died of AIDS." I said it in a whisper. He said, "You don't have to whisper to me." And he came around the counter and hugged me.

And I didn't know him, but I loved him.

March 3, 2004

FIRE
and
WATER

In July 2005 we opened our second permanent booth in New York City at the World Trade Center site. This booth is available to the general public, and it has special slots reserved for families to remember loved ones lost on September 11, 2001, as well as for rescue workers and survivors. While the vast majority of StoryCorps participants come in pairs, 9/11 families frequently come alone and the facilitator asks the questions. Soon after we opened, facilitators began referring to their work with 9/11 families as "bearing witness."

In September 2006, New York City mayor Michael Bloomberg announced that StoryCorps would become the first collection documenting the lives lost on September 11 to be placed in the World Trade Center Memorial Museum when it

StoryCorps Booth at the World Trade Center site

opens in 2010. We also announced a joint effort with the museum to record at least one story for each person who perished in the attacks.

Tommy Sullivan was eating breakfast at Windows on the World restaurant on the top of World Trade Center Tower One on the morning of September 11, 2001. His sister, Norene, and his mother, Arlene, were the first participants to record an interview in our Ground Zero booth. One year later, in September 2006, Norene spoke at the announcement of our partnership with the museum:

> My mother was bestowed the honor of being the first person interviewed at this booth, followed by my aunt,

where I had the pleasure of asking the questions both times. Today, Mom is smiling and laughing more. Can I say the booth was the reason? Not entirely. But it was surely the beginning. The talking began there. The healing began there. Both interviews were finished in what felt like minutes. Once we got started, the conversations just flowed. It was an incredible experience.

We talked about the things we loved most about Tommy. We laughed about the good times we had and the funny things my brother used to say and do, and we talked about what a great person he was. You must be thinking, "What's so extraordinary about that?" Nothing, really. People do that all the time. And, yes, you are correct if you're thinking that you don't need to go to this booth to do that. But we had tough conversations in there, things everyone wants to talk about but doesn't. I learned a lot about my mother and my aunt that day, and although I talk to them all the time, it wasn't like in there.

In the aftermath of September 11, you could not walk past a person without greeting them. We didn't honk our horns impatiently at each other. We wished each other a safe trip home and a peaceful weekend. Five years later, we are right back where we were on September 10, 2001. But to me it's worse—because we should know better. Somehow we lost that connection we had. I believe this booth can give it back to us.

I learned a valuable lesson from my mother that day, and I will pass along her wisdom to you: Tell the people you love that you love them every day. You never know when you won't see them again.

In late 2005, StoryCorps spent three weeks in Gulfport, Mississippi, and in May 2006 spent a month in New Orleans recording interviews with survivors of Hurricane Katrina, one of the worst catastrophes ever to strike the United States. What follows are stories from two of the most significant moments in twenty-first-century American history: September 11, 2001, and Hurricane Katrina in August 2005.

RICHARD PECORELLA, 53, remembers his fiancée, KAREN JUDAY, with facilitator JACKIE GOODRICH

RECORDED IN NEW YORK CITY

Richard Pecorella: Karen Juday is my fiancée's name. We met four and a half years prior to 9/11 at a car race in Nazareth, Pennsylvania. A friend of mine gave me tickets. He says, "Why don't you go to an Indy car race?" He says, "Get out of New York. This divorce thing is killing you. Just go. Have a good time."

I went to the race and sat down and I'm looking around. And all of a sudden Karen comes in and sits down next to me. She had a dungaree dress on, blond, curly hair, big smile. Sits down next to me, and she says, "Hello." I said, "How ya doing?" She said, "How'd you get these tickets?" Because it was the owner of the racetrack's seats. So I says, "Oh, a friend of mine on Wall Street gave them to me." She says, "Oh, you work on Wall Street?" I say, "Yeah. It's my first car race." "Your first car race? You've never been to one?" I said, "Nope." "Oh, I'll tell you all about it." So she explained the whole thing. Then she told me about her brother being Al Unser Jr.'s mechanic, and he was down working in the pits, and that's why she was in Pennsylvania.

She was from Elkhart, Indiana. She was telling me about her life, how she was born on a farm and she had a pet calf. And she'd been there all her life, and she was a supervisor in an assembly line making amplifiers for rock groups. I said, "Oh, that's interesting." She says, "It's a life." She says, "I'm in the middle of a separation from my second husband." I say, "Oh, I'm in the middle of a divorce. Maybe you'd like to go to dinner after the race?" She looks at me, she goes, "You know what? Maybe I will."

So she found this steakhouse and for the life of me I can't remember the name of the place. And I should. We went to the restaurant, and on the way I saw a gas station that sold roses. So I pull in to the gas station and say, "Wait here a minute." I ran in and got a dozen roses, brought them back to the car, I said, "Here, these are for you." And her eyes just lit up. "Nobody ever gave me flowers before!" And she had tears in her eyes. I said, "You got to be kidding me." She goes, "I'm telling you the truth—nobody ever gave me flowers." I said, "Well, that's a mistake on their part."

We went to the restaurant, and almost through the whole meal I don't think I ate a bite—and I'm not shy from eating. I had my hands holding her hands across the table the whole time. I mean, I just can't describe it—clasped together across the middle of the table. We exchanged telephone numbers, and the next morning she was going back to Indiana, and that evening I was going back to Brooklyn. And I'm saying to myself, "What am I going to do here? This is the love of my life I'm letting go!" I knew it that day that we met. I knew as soon as I looked at her that she was the one. It was magical. I can't describe it. I couldn't tell her that, but I was like a fifteen-year-old again. I got all google-eyed and didn't know what to do or say, and stumbling. It wasn't like me at all. Wasn't the typical macho Italian guy from Brooklyn. (*Laughs.*) I could see she was a little goo-goo also. Her eyes were sparkling. She didn't want me to leave; she didn't want to go home to Indiana.

Four days later she calls me up on the phone at work and says, "Richard," she says, "I'm packing up and moving in with my brother in Pennsylvania so we can see each other on the weekends." She says, "I just want to be able to get to know you." I was shocked. I said, "How can you do that, just pack up and leave your whole life? You're in Elkhart, Indiana. You were born and raised there and work there." She says, "I've lived my life. My children are grown up. There's nothing for me here. I want to go for it." I said, "I can't make you any promises." And she said, "I'm going." I said, "Okay." She packed up, and that evening she drove to Pennsylvania. I left work and met her out there, got to meet her brother and sister for the first time. And I stayed that weekend, and then we alternated weekends: One weekend she'd come to Brooklyn, then I'd go back to Pennsylvania. When my divorce was finalized, I asked her to move in with me, and she was there the next day with her car packed. It was amazing. I can't describe how it was. It was magical.

To me, she looked like Norma Jean—not Marilyn Monroe the actress, Norma Jean before the actress. She had blondish hair and always wanted to wear a dress; she didn't like wearing pants. I guess she was pretty old-fashioned in that sense. Even her work ethic. We got her a job at Cantor Fitzgerald. A friend of mine was director of operations, and he needed a secretary, and she happened to be good on a computer only because the assembly line she worked on was automated so she had to use a computer. He couldn't believe her work ethic. She says, "I came here to work. I'm not here to fool around." She says, "You get a job, you get paid for it, you have to do the job."

She changed me as I changed her. I was a very stressed person. I was in a messy divorce. I had an ex-wife who I was battling with over money, and so I needed a little anger management. And when I met Karen, somehow she just relaxed me. She told me, "It's not worth it. You'll get through it. The divorce is done now." And she showed me how to live in a city of stress without the stress.

And in turn I showed her New York. This is a woman who never saw an ocean until she came to New York. When she came over the Verrazano Bridge, she says, "I'm in love with this bridge." She asked me what that waterway was there; I said, "It's the Atlantic Ocean." And she just became a New Yorker almost within weeks of her moving there. It wasn't anything that she imagined from what she saw on TV. She said it's like a small town only just everybody's closer together. There's more people and more buildings, but other than that it was a small town to her. And she just showed me how to appreciate what I had here.

I wanted to get married almost as soon as she moved in with me. And she told me my children weren't ready for it. I had two grown daughters in their twenties, and she said, "They're not ready. When they're ready, we'll get married. There's no reason for us to get married." And I couldn't believe it, because most of the time it's the woman that wants to get married and the guy backs away. She taught me patience. I had very little patience. Again, I was a tough guy from Brooklyn, grew up on the streets, went to work, worked my way up in the company. And basically I was one of those guys who rolled down the window, screamed at the drivers when they weren't driving the way I thought they should be. And she toned me down. She showed me how to be nicer to people, give it a second thought before you start yelling. And I've carried that with me. She didn't sit down and teach it to me; it was just by her actions that I followed.

She was very spontaneous. Any time we did a driving trip, it was always an adventure—even a short trip. We would go to her brother's house quite often. It was a two-hour drive, and one of the things we used to do became a joke later on. We would get frisky in the car and would decide to stop at a motel along the way, and, you know, we were both forty-something years old at the time. And her brother would be waiting for us to get there in two hours, and we wouldn't get there for five hours. You know, we said, "Well, what the hell? They can wait for us!" (*Laughs.*)

But our best trips were to Las Vegas. She loved it there, and I loved it there. We just got back from there two days before she was killed, and we were going to get married there the following June. I'm going to need a moment. . . .

September 11—that morning we actually were not even supposed to come to work. My mother was supposed to get knee surgery, and the night before, the doctor canceled the surgery because her blood pressure was up. So Karen said, "Well, let's go to work then." I said, "We already got the day off. Why don't—" She says, "Nah, let's go in. Why waste it?"

And every morning Karen would drive with me to my office, and then she'd take the subway from my office one stop to the Trade Center. I worked in Brooklyn, across the river from the Trade Center. So it was a typical morning. Drove to the train station, dropped her off, kissed her good-bye, said, "I love you." She went to the office, and my office actually faced the World Trade Center. So from my window across the East River, I could see the Twin Towers.

So I'm doing some work, and one of my workers comes in and says, "Richie, I just heard that the Trade Center got hit with a plane." I wasn't looking out the window. I turn around, and I see the building burning. I said, "Oh my God!" I got on the phone, and I start calling her. Phone rings, no answer. I call her cell phone. I get her voicemail. And I run down to another guy's office who had a better angle on the building, and I'm looking and I'm saying, "It's right around what floor she was on." She was on the 101st floor. I said, "Maybe she's going to go down the stairs. It looks like it's a little below her." And I kept calling the phone, and as I'm watching, I see this other plane coming around the bend. I said, "What the hell is that?" I thought it was a rescue plane or a reconnaissance plane coming to look to see what took place. And then all of a sudden it turned, and it dove into the building. And that's when I knew that we were being attacked, and I just went, "Oh my God. This is no accident!"

I screamed, and I ran to try and get out of the building, and the guy who was in the office said, "Richard, stay here!" They're restraining me now, trying to keep me there, and I said, "No, I got to get over there! I got to get over there!" Security came, and they brought me back to my office. And the first building collapses. I took my office chair, and I threw it at my window. I wanted to get out, but nobody would let me out. They had two security guards outside my office.

So now I collapsed on the floor, and I'm trembling, you know, I'm going into shock. So they brought the nurse up; they put me in my chair. The nurse says, "Sit down." She gives me a bottle of water, and my hand is trembling so much that it's splashing all over me. I couldn't even hold the bottle in my hand. And the nurse says, "I want to take your blood pressure." I says, "You ain't taking my blood pressure! My girlfriend was just murdered!" This is what they told me I said. And then I just passed out in my chair.

They woke me up and told me my daughter's here, and they said, "Rich, maybe she got out. You know it's chaos over there." But I saw what took place. The only hope I had was if she was downstairs having a cigarette when the plane hit. But obviously that wasn't it, so my daughter took me home. I remember very little of that. They said I was on the floor flipping and screaming. I just kept seeing the plane hitting the building.

From that point on, when her brother got there, we just went into the city and were searching hospitals and the morgue, trying to find out anything. Then we went through all of Manhattan and all of Brooklyn posting her picture, hoping that a doctor or a nurse might have seen her in a hospital— even though I really knew that she was gone. I knew she didn't get out, because she would have called me. She was a very strong woman, and she was very strong-willed, and she was in very good shape. So if she got out, she would have somehow gotten to notify me.

I think it took about thirty-six hours before I said there's no sense going to the hospitals and the morgues anymore. When the city announced that it was on a recovery mission, we said, "There's no more searching. Where are we going to go?"

I think the biggest thing that helped me was going to the Cantor [Fitzgerald] grieving center and meeting with the other families and seeing the devastation that other families had. One of Karen's bosses, he had four sons under the age of ten. There were thirteen hundred children that lost one parent or both at Cantor. There were mothers and fathers who lost both their kids. Cantor didn't have a nepotism rule, so if you were related, you could work there—so there were so many people that lost multiple kids, and so many kids that lost multiple parents. Cantor lost 658 people. So I started looking at it. I lost the love of my life, but look at the devastation that happened here.

There's no cemetery plot. They found some DNA, but it was nothing that we could put in a casket or bury. We dropped her ashes over the Verrazano Bridge. That was her favorite place. And I would like to get a plaque put on a fence over there one day, but the city won't allow me to do it. So maybe one day when they're not around I'll put it up. (*Laughs.*)

I miss her eyes. Her eyes sparkled to me. They were just— One day they were blue, next day they were green, depending on how the light hit them. She was just always, always smiling when we were together. Other than her going to work, there wasn't a time we weren't together. We would walk to the store together; it wasn't "You go to the store." If we had to go somewhere, it was always together.

Karen, I love you. I always will. I feel your presence all the time. I just hope you keep guiding me in the right direction. I lost my soul. I still have my heart, but I lost my soul. Karen, I'll always be in love with you; there will never be another one. And I will see you again. I will do enough good to make it up there to be with you.

July 29, 2005

. . . .

JOSEPH DITTMAR, 47, interviewed by
facilitator RANI SHANKAR, 28

RECORDED IN CHICAGO, ILLINOIS

Joseph Dittmar: I'm here today in Chicago to tell a story about surviving on September 11, 2001. I'm in the insurance industry, and New York City, and in particular the World Trade Center, has always been a mecca for the insurance industry. Being in that business, it was not unusual for myself or any of us to be in New York for a meeting. I started the morning of September 11, actually, in South Jersey. I got up at 3:30 in the morning to drive to Philadelphia, to take a Metroliner from Philly to New York City. As we were approaching the station in Newark, New Jersey, my cell phone rang. It woke me, and it was my wife back in Chicago. I said, "I'm glad you called. You woke me up. The train is pulling in to Newark, and it's a lot easier to get to where I'm going from Newark." She said, "I thought you were going to New York." I said, "Yes, but I'm going to the Trade Center, so it's just a lot easier to take the PATH over from Newark." So I told my wife that morning, kind of by accident, that I was going to the Trade Center.

I got off the train in Newark and took the PATH train over to Two World Trade Center, where we were going to meet at Aon Corporation's headquarters, which were on the 105th floor. Mary Wieman was the facilitator of the meeting.

Mary was a broker for Aon Corporation and somebody that we had all known for quite some time—a very powerful woman. So it was really hysterical when we got up to this 105th-floor conference room, and there's Mary with a bottle of liquid soap dusting furniture. Way out of character for Mary; this was not something that she would normally do. But this was an important meeting for her. She wanted the place to look good.

At about 8:30, when the meeting was supposed to begin, virtually all the fifty-four attendees were there. We were in an enclosed conference room with no windows to the outside world. At about 8:48, the lights flickered. That's all. No sound of any sort, no sight of anything. Just the lights flickered. Nobody thought a whole lot about it. Almost immediately a gentleman by the name of Rick Blood walked into the room. He looked at everybody and said, "Hey, I'm a volunteer fire marshal for the 105th, 104th, and 103rd floors here in the Trade Center at Aon, and there's been an explosion in the North Tower and we've got to evacuate." Everybody in the room looked at Rick and kind of waved their hands. A couple people grumbled. The attitude was generally "Hey, we're here for a meeting, and we're fine. Nothing's going on. Let us go." I remember thinking to myself, "Damn, I came all the way here for this meeting, and now we're going to evacuate." It was just a feeling of aggravation more than anything. Everybody grabbed for their left or right hip so they could call and groan and moan to somebody about the fact that this meeting was potentially going to get canceled. Interestingly enough, the cells weren't working. We didn't know why not at that point. We were soon to find out, but nobody could really get out on a cell phone and make a call.

When everybody was moaning and groaning, Rick said, "Hey, look, I can't leave until everybody leaves, and I want to leave." He said it with a smile, and that got everybody to get up and go. They herded us all down to the closest fire escape on the 105th floor to get out of the building. Nobody knew what was going on. When we got down to the 90th floor, the door to the fire stairwell was propped open. Now if you've ever been in a high-rise building, you know that if you look on the back of those doors, you'll see a sign that says something like "Once you're in here, don't leave here. Go all the way down and exit at the lobby level." And here was this door propped open on the 90th floor, and everybody's herding out that door. I did what everybody else did. I followed them out. I should've known better, but I kept thinking to myself, "Hey, I don't know the building. Maybe I have to go to another fire escape somewhere and make a switch." I wasn't sure what was going on or why everybody was going out.

As soon as I got on the 90th floor, it became pretty evident what people were doing. It wound up being probably the thirty to forty worst seconds of my life because that was the first opportunity we had to see the North Tower in an unbelievable state of tumult. The plumes of smoke five, six, seven stories high. Flames redder than anything you've seen before, and the fire just spilling out of the building. It was a beautiful, clear day, and we clearly saw through the smoke and flames the signs of a fuselage of the plane. Being such a clear day, I remember immediately thinking, "God, how could this person have missed?" We saw the paper and the furniture and the people falling from the building, and it was an unbelievably gruesome sight. People on the 90th floor seemed to be almost mesmerized by this. People were screaming, "Oh my God! Oh my God!" and every time we'd see somebody fall from the building, there'd be another shriek. And yet these people seemed to be just pressed to the glass to watch. I never got that close. I can't even watch a horror movie—and to see something like this. . . . You know this wasn't a made-for-TV movie—this was real life, and it scared me. And I thought to myself, "I'm not going to stay here."

Two really strong feelings took over my whole being at that time. One just made me go, "I want to get the hell out of here." But the other feeling that came over me almost immediately, as I'm seeing this gruesome sight through the window, was the feeling that I know everybody has. It's called the "I want my mommy" feeling. I just wanted to go home. So I don't know— maybe I'm a big coward, but at that point I said, "I can't watch this anymore. I have to leave. I have to get out of here." As I turned to go back to the fire escape, one of the guys that was in the meeting said, "What are you going to do?" I said, "I'm going to get the hell out of here. What are you going to do?" And he said he was going to get out, too, but he explained to me that before he was going to go down ninety more flights of steps, he was going to go to the restroom. This guy made a simple decision—to go to the restroom—and he didn't get out that day.

I got back in the fire escape, and it was right at that point when the PA systems started to make the infamous announcement that said something to the effect of: "The event has been contained to the North Tower. The South Tower is safe. If you work in this building, we suggest that you go back to your workstation. If you're a visitor, we suggest that you stay where you are until further notice, but if you do feel you need to leave, please proceed with caution." I didn't hesitate. I was leaving, and I proceeded with caution. But it was absolutely incredible to see the number of people in that stairwell who turned around at the 90th and proceeded to go back up to where they worked.

I decided that I was going home. I wasn't going to stay. I had to leave. I was somewhere between the 75th and the 70th floor when the second plane plowed into our building. I've never felt anything like that before, and I hope I never do again in my life. That stairwell literally shook from side to side—what seemed like 30- and 40-degree angles. This building was rocking back and forth. The concrete was breaking—the handrails breaking away from the concrete. The steps were waves undulating underneath our feet. Unbelievable. There was this heat ball that went blowing by us faster than I can say it, and you could smell the jet fuel. And it seemed like it was going on for hours, but it was probably seconds or minutes. I was able to stay on my feet while this thing rocked back and forth. It's unbelievable how strong that building actually was to be able to take that. We didn't have a clue that our building had been struck.

About a flight and a half of steps later, I caught up with Fred and Todd, the guys that I came into the meeting with that morning, and Fred was kind of picking himself up. Todd had already gotten up from falling down, and they were dusting themselves off and getting themselves together. And you know what was weird—you would think when something like this had just happened, there would be all this screaming and panic and pandemonium. But actually the best way to describe it was just stunned silence. People had no clue. Once again people were trying to use their cells, but their cells were gone. Actually, that probably was a good thing, because I think if we were able to call the people that we wanted to reach, the ones that we cared about the most—in my instance, my wife—it would have probably scared us more than helped us, because the people that were not in the building knew exactly what was going on. People were watching this live on television. We were in a concrete tower, and we had no clue. In our wildest dreams we never thought that a plane had come into our building.

I found out later on that the heat just from the friction of the plane through the building was over 2,000 degrees Fahrenheit. So all those people on the 78th floor, they didn't know what hit them. I guess that's a good thing, because there was no pain for them. (*Crying.*)

Even after the plane hit our building, the lights were on and some type of ventilation was working because we were getting air in that tower, and we weren't getting any smoke other than that heat ball that flew by us and that little bit of jet fuel smell.

We figured out later that we started on the 105th floor, the highest occupied floor in the building that day, so basically there was nobody behind us. There just weren't that many people there. That was another reason why I don't think there was a lot of panic.

Fred had ripped his pants and suit when he had fallen down, and it was starting to get warm because we were huffing and puffing down a lot of steps. Fred had smoked in his earlier days, and it caught up with him. He had half a lung removed, so he was really struggling. He walked down two or three flights of steps, and he kind of wanted to quit. He'd say, "You guys go ahead." We wouldn't let him do that. We would coach and coax each other down. And we saw some people that were either a little bit overweight or partially handicapped, and we were trying to encourage them, "Come on. You can do it." They were wanting to quit, and we couldn't necessarily help by carrying them. What we could do was we could encourage them. We couldn't run, so you kind of do this little skip thing going down the steps, to try to move as quickly as you can. We had never seen so many pairs of women's shoes in one place. It was absolutely incredible. But when you think about it, if you've got heels that are six inches tall and you're trying to go down seventy-eight flights of steps, you're certainly not going to wear those shoes. So the shoes got zapped off to the side, and we were just kicking them out of the way

It wasn't until the 35th floor that we finally got a good sense of what was going on, because that was the first chance we had to run into the firefighters, the police, and the paramedics. It's hard to talk about because we realized, after the fact, that the looks on their faces— They knew exactly what was going on. They knew that they were going into basically the bowels of hell, and they knew they were not going to get out. They knew, and yet here they are, going up those steps. Unbelievable. I thank them for saving all those lives that day. I mean, three thousand people lost their lives, but thousands and thousands of people were saved. We owe those guys. We owe them not to ever forget.

We saw a guy that had been walking along with us—he was a maintenance guy from the building—and the whole time he had with him one of those phones that act like walkie-talkies. And right at the time we saw the firefighters and the police, this thing started to belch and beep and make all kinds of electronic noises—and we hear this voice screaming through the phone, "We're on eighty-two. I can't get down. I can't get down. We don't know what we're going to do!" And this guy stopped, turned around, and started to go back up the steps. He was right next to me, and I looked at him and said, "What are you going to do?" He said, "I don't know, man, but I got to go help my friend." If you want to know what an American hero is, that maintenance man is the true American hero. I mean, this guy was willing to throw away his life to save that of a friend. Just to be able to do that—the guts, the bravery, and the grit—the love of another human being, it was hard to watch. I can only hope that guy got turned around by the cops and the firefighters later on.

Probably my favorite character was on the 15th floor, but we heard him on the 18th floor. It was a security guard, and he was singing. I mean he was singing at the top of his lungs, and he was singing "God Bless America," which was an unusual pick of a song, or so we thought. And he's singing this as loud as he can in this off-tone way and kind of messing up the words. In the middle of the singing he'd stop and he'd yell, "This is a day you'll never forget!" And then he'd sing a little bit more real loud, and then he'd stop and say, "This is a day that's going to go down in history! And you'll be a part of it!" He just kept going on, and, you know, it was incredible. This was another guy that knew. He was sent up from probably the lobby level to get to the 15th floor, to make sure that people kept moving down that stairwell. And it was kind of like the thing in the *Titanic* where they put the musicians up on the deck to keep people calm. This guy was singing and making cracks and making people laugh and making people think he's crazy, and what he was really doing is keeping people calm and saving lives. Incredible. Absolutely incredible.

When we got down to the lobby level, Fred went out of the door first, and he looked back at me and he said, "Hey, don't look left and don't look right." And when someone tells you to do that, you look left and right. And I saw the carnage, the twisted steel, the concrete, the red blotches—and we knew what the red blotches were. It was absolutely a horrific sight. It was like the ravages of war.

We were following the crowd—nobody really directing us in any particular way. They were pushing stuff back away from the building with little Bobcat bulldozers. It was just gruesome to see what was on the ground. The cops were yelling at us, "Don't look back—just go. Run, run, run." You know, like Sodom and Gomorrah, somebody's telling you not to look back. You look back, and you see these buildings in an unbelievable state of duress. It was incredible, absolutely incredible to see these buildings so torn apart.

We were about eight blocks north of the building at a commercial laundry whose doors were open. We wanted to use their phone. They had their radio on, and they had the all-news stations on, and that was the first opportunity we had to hear that this was an on-purpose terrorist attack, and our jaws just dropped to the ground. I remember thinking, "Not here, not in the States. This could never happen!" It was right at that time that the two sounds that haunt me every day occurred. First, the sound of the twisting steel and crumbling concrete, and the building that we were just in—the South Tower—falling to the ground. But the sound that haunts me the most is the sound that I hear before I go to sleep at night and when I wake up in the morning: the sound of millions of people on the streets of New York all screaming a bloodcurdling scream at the same time.

We got out of New York that day by pure luck. I got on a train that left the city to go to Philly. When we came out from under the Hudson and looked back to see what was that beautiful skyline—just a pile of smoke. It was an eighty-minute trip from New York to Philly, and there was not a word in the crowded train. Not a word was spoken. It was just a stunned silence.

I took a rental car to my mom and dad's house, who still live in Philly. There was my mom to meet me on the steps of the house, giving me this big hug and a kiss. I basically did what everybody else did that night. I went into that house and watched TV to try to understand what was going on. I passed out from pure exhaustion and trauma.

Got up the next morning and made the fourteen-hour trip to Illinois in about eleven and a half hours. I called everybody—anybody that cared to talk to me and that I thought I needed to talk to, every member of my family, even cousins, aunts, and uncles that I hadn't talked to in a long time. Word traveled fast. My mom and my wife had basically been able to tell everybody where I'd been and what had occurred, and it was just good to talk to people, because there was a security feeling—that people cared. You find out who your friends are and who really loves you on days like that.

As I got closer to Aurora, Illinois, where I lived at that time, I called my wife for about the thousandth time and I said, "Where are you?" She said, "I'm just getting ready to go to church because they're having a Mass. I'll just wait for you if you're getting close." I said, "No, no, today's a good day to go to church. It's a good place to be." And I said, "I'll meet you there." I drove up into the parking lot of the church and walked into the back of the church and opened the door to the main church area. This place was just packed. These hundreds of people in the church were all staring back at me because they had known what had occurred. I looked over to the right—to the pew where we always sit, and there was my wife, and there were my kids and my family and my friends.

My wife's real nondemonstrative, real quiet, and she jumped over the back of the pew and ran to the back of the church and gave me this gigantic hug and kiss.

And I knew that I was home. I was home.

August 19, 2004

. . . .

Pump operators **RUFUS BURKHALTER,**
61, and BOBBY BROWN, 58, talk about
their work at the Sewerage and Water Board
of New Orleans, where they have been
employed for more than twenty years

RECORDED IN NEW ORLEANS, LOUISIANA

Rufus Burkhalter: For people who don't know what a
pumping station is, it's similar to the dams in Holland. We sit
below sea level, and we pump our water uphill. And here in
this city we have these big old motor-operated pumps. And it's
essential for the city of New Orleans to have these things because we sit below sea level.

Bobby Brown: And to better understand that, for those who
are naïve to what we're saying, we're like a saucer surrounded
by water, which is above us, so we're pumping water out of the
saucer, up and over the top.

Rufus: Pumping uphill. And some people think we only
pump water when it rains or during the hurricane season. But
we pump water every day because if we stop pumping water,
this city would automatically flood out from people washing
their vehicles, washing their dishes, using their toilet—simply
because we sit below sea level.

So when a hurricane comes, we got to be on the ball. We
got to be Johnny-on-the-spot to make sure that that water
don't flood out the city. We pump water out of the city into

Lake Pontchartrain. And they got levies down the side of the canal that hold that water.

I've been a pump operator for twenty, twenty-one years. During Katrina, during the night of the storm, I was at the helms. I was the operator that was pumping. And you was kind of my backup when the storm hit that night. Was it devastating to you?

Bobby: Well, at the time it wasn't devastating because we were watching the track of the storm. It looked like we were going to be on the dry side, that it wasn't going to be that bad for us. We've worked with these hurricanes, and in most cases the worst was over within two or three days. So I was in that frame of mind for Katrina. Two or three days this thing will be over with and then everything will go back to normal. But as we all know, it didn't turn out that way.

Rufus: We was sitting at the station, and the winds was picking up pretty good. I think it was that Monday, sometime early that morning, when we lost our electricity. But we were still doing our job because we had pumps available through another source of electricity. We didn't panic. Until six o'clock that evening, when we—

Bobby: Discovered—

Rufus: You and I was outside when we discovered that breach. We was walking around to the back of the station when that water started coming. It was coming so fast, it started filling up the entire station and the basement, and that's where we keep our transformers, electrical switch gear. And with the water—

Bobby: Coming up so fast—

Rufus: We would have been blown up if that water would have hit those transformers. And usually to kill that power source in that station, with all those feeders and things, it takes about an hour or so. But we did that in less than five, ten minutes.

Bobby: We didn't panic. We had to go into survival mode. The power to the pump was cut off. What function does the pumping station have when it's got no power?

Rufus: None. None whatsoever. We was just there, and the water was rising. And even if we had power, pumping the water wouldn't have done any good because the levee had breached and the water was coming from the lake. We would have been doing nothing but circulating the water right back to us if we continued to pump. If the levee would have held steadfast, then we could have pumped the water out of the city.

Bobby: How many days did we stay after the power went out?

Rufus: Four days. We left on the fourth day. We were still trying to get at least one or two pumps to start pumping and was praying that the Corps of Engineers would put sandbags or something to block the breach in the levees so we could pump the water out of the city. We were still trying to do our job.

You remember, I was going to look for one of my nephews because he works in the sewer department, and I was trying to find him. And on our way down there, I thought I was dreaming for a while. I thought I saw bodies, dead bodies, laying in the water and floating.

Bobby: I don't believe that was no dream.

Rufus: That kind of took a toll on me. They put in the paper it was all elderly people, but they had babies that drowned in that hurricane. That took a toll on me. And I don't know if you remember, after that when we found that store open. I hadn't taken a drink in seventeen years. And I took— It overtook me. I was the deacon in church, and I started drinking. And I was wondering why.

Bobby: Yeah, well, I know because I was there with you. But you survived it, and you was able to get out that bottle and get your head back on straight. People deal with catastrophes. You saw people dead, floating in the water. But, you know, even at that, we stayed together, and we did what we had to do to try and protect this city and do our jobs.

Rufus: As a matter of fact, if this city would ever go under, we would be the last people here—either die or we'd be the last ones to leave because that's what our jobs demand.

Bobby: It came to the point where there was nothing else we could do, and it came upon us to evacuate ourselves. But, you know, even at that, we did what we had to do to try and protect this city and do our jobs. People just don't realize what we went through.

Rufus: It's going to linger with us. It's going to be with us. I'll be sixty-two on the twentieth of June. And for the rest of my life I know it's going to linger. It's gonna be there with me.

May 14, 2006

*Bobby Brown (l.) and
Rufus Burkhalter (r.)*

DOUGLAS PAUL DESILVEY, 59,
interviewed by facilitator
NICK YULMAN, 25

RECORDED IN GULFPORT, MISSISSIPPI

Douglas Paul deSilvey: The story that I want to tell today is about my family. I'll start with my daughter, Donna. Donna was quite remarkable. She was thirty-five years of age. Donna was an entrepreneur and didn't let nothing stand in her way. My wife, Linda, who was Donna's mother, was a social worker in Biloxi. And Linda was the type of person that was always caring for someone. She was a giving lady, and she would look out for other folks before she looked out for herself. Nadine was Donna's grandmother and Linda's mother. Nadine was a businesswoman—an interior decorator. And Ted, her husband, was an accomplished clarinet player on the Gulf Coast for many years. Ted was a good man and was good to Nadine.

On Sunday we went over to Nadine and Ted's home in Ocean Springs to prepare for the storm. Not knowing what we were in for, we considered it just another storm. Every time we had a hurricane, we would all go to Nadine's. They were both up in age, and we went over to support them, because Nadine didn't want to leave like most of the elderly folks. And I would prepare the home for wind and rain and get the place boarded up and get the generators, sandbag the garage doors, get food and water—just the normal things that you do for a hurricane.

This was Nadine's retirement home. It was two stories, eighteen feet above sea level, a totally brick home. It had steel beams throughout the structure to compensate for the wind and rain—knowing it would be susceptible to hurricanes. Since '77, when she built this house, we've been through every storm in it and never had the first problem. I boarded the house up. I went home and got Donna and Linda, and we brought everything over there, and we bedded down for the night and got everything ready for the next day, when the storm was supposed to come on land.

Monday morning we had breakfast, and everything was pretty much normal. I was keeping an eye on things—where the water was, how fast it was coming up—just things I always did. Normal drill for a hurricane. Nadine and Ted went up to their bedrooms; my wife, Linda, and I and my daughter, Donna, stayed downstairs watching TV and cleaning up the dishes.

Within an hour the water just came up so fast that it was unbelievable. When the water started coming in the garage and the den area, Donna and I were packing towels underneath it. And just instantly the back door burst open. Now, I had these doors covered with three-eighths-inch plywood. Everything just burst off the hinges toward the den, and instantly the place was just full of water. I couldn't believe how fast it was coming in. I told Donna to get her mother and get upstairs into Nadine's bedroom, which was the most structurally sound part of the whole house. We were sitting on the bed, and I could hear glass breaking, and, of course, I had an idea of what was going on outside her bedroom—but I had no idea what was about to happen.

I walked from the front of her bedroom to the back, which was facing the bay, just to see how high the water was, and in the back she has three 35-foot palm trees, and they were totally under water. I couldn't see the tops of them at all. I said we were going to have to get into the water and not try to swim but grab something and float with it. Go with the tide, don't try to go against it, and, above all, stay together.

As I turned and told them to hold hands, I heard a noise, and the roof came up. I could see daylight. Then the walls came down, and as the roof came back down, there were no walls to support it. The last thing I remember seeing was Donna reaching for her mother. *(Crying.)* I was heading towards them to try to get them out of there, and the roof came down on all of us. The only reason I'm here now is because I was at the back of the room, where there was just enough air to breathe. My lungs started filling up with water, but I kept asking Jesus not to let me go like this. I had to get my family out. And I'm a big guy—I'm 268 pounds, and I exercise and stay healthy—and I just could not do a thing. They were gone.

I was on this pile of debris, and it started floating towards a magnolia tree. And as it went by the magnolia tree, I grabbed ahold of one of the limbs. And all of a sudden there was all four of their bodies floating in the water. I couldn't do a thing. I didn't get a chance to tell them I loved them. And they were gone. *(Crying.)*

I guess I went into shock. I jumped into the water, and I realized I had to tell the authorities what happened so they could get them out of there before the night. I got in the water and went up to higher ground. Walked another four or five miles to find somebody, and there was a house on fire, and the fire department was there. And I told them what happened and I needed a sheriff right away. So they got him, and he asked me, "How do you know that they're dead?" I said, "They were floating in the water. Everybody was facedown. All I could see was their backs." And (*crying*) he said he'd get 'em out. Then they called somebody to take me home.

We got to my house and saw that all I had was roof damage. So I stayed there that night and realized that I had no water. Nothing to eat, because we'd taken most of the dried goods over to Nadine's because we figured we'd need them the next day. So I took five Aleve and drank some—I think I had some milk or something in the refrigerator to get it down. And I sat down on my chair and passed out and got up the next morning.

I stopped by Bill Dellenger's house, and he asked me if I heard about the people that died down by Nadine's house. I said, "Bill, that was Nadine and Ted and Linda and Donna. All four of them drowned. I almost drowned myself." And Bill fainted. I stopped at Home Depot, and I bought enough one-by-fours to make crosses. I put their names on them, their date of birth, what they were known for, and went back over there the next day. In front of Nadine's home was a beam that came from part of her house. I nailed those four crosses to that beam across the driveway, just so people would know what happened. I wanted to uphold their memories and their names and what they stood for.

Linda and Nadine and Donna—the three women in my

family who steered my life to the man that I am today. And I hope and think that I am a pretty good fellow. They all believed in me and supported me and backed me up on everything I ever attempted. You just won't find three women like that again. Very special.

The biggest problem I have now in dealing with this situation is going to sleep at night. *(Crying.)* Losing a family is—I don't think there's any words for it. As a dad and a husband, you always plan for the future of everybody, and you always plan for you not being there one day—making sure your family is taken care of, and insurance on the house and Donna's college and everything's paid for. I've always looked out for them and made sure that they had what they needed. I guess I just did what a dad does. Well, it's just the opposite now. I have nobody to plan for—it's just me. So it kind of makes you wonder what life is all about.

These days I wake up and go to my office and do my job. I have nobody to come home to, and it's just me to worry about. I've got the house full of their belongings that I don't know what to do about. I just go to work and come home.

I spoke to my daughter every day on the phone, and there's a few words that parents take for granted. You know, like "Hey, Dad, what's going on?" "Hey, Dad, how was your day today?" "Hey, Dad, could you send me a hundred dollars? I'm short on the rent." You know, stuff like that. I'll never hear "Hey, Dad" again.

What's keeping me going is the pictures that I have. I'm kind of a camera nut. I enjoy taking pictures, and they're worth more now than anything in the world. And you just don't realize something like that until the people are gone. So the pictures and the little things that I have in the house that belonged to them, that's what's getting me through it.

I've got a lot of folks that are concerned about me, so between them and my faith, I'll get through this and be a better man. I can't let this beat me.

December 8, 2005

- - - - - - - - - - - -

KIERSTA KURTZ-BURKE, 37,
interviewed by her husband,
JUSTIN LUNDGREN, 36

RECORDED IN NEW ORLEANS, LOUISIANA

Justin Lundgren: How is it that you ended up going to Charity Hospital when Katrina hit?

Kiersta Kurtz-Burke: We're on call every six weeks, so that was my weekend on call. Saturday was pretty uneventful. I went in and saw the patients at Charity and rounded with my resident. And at the end of the time I was there, we were talking a little bit about the storm coming toward New Orleans. But to be honest, we were so wrapped up in our patients, it didn't really register to me.

Sunday night the wind started to really kick up, and one of the building supervisors came around at about ten o'clock and said, "You know the windows in this building will shatter at more than seventy-five miles per hour." And the winds were already about seventy miles per hour. So that was the first inkling I had that something could go terribly wrong.

A few windows shattered on upper floors. None of the windows on our floor shattered, but the water started coming in horizontally under our windowpanes. Suddenly we were dealing with one to two inches of water on the floor, including patient rooms. We used every towel and sheet we had on the floor, not knowing that we would never have clean laundry again, which we really regretted later on.

At 6:00 A.M. Monday, the storm was still really going on, but it was kind of the tail end of it as we understood, and we still had TV, we still had power. At around six or six-thirty in the morning, my resident and I decided we would do rounds as usual. We had gotten all the water cleaned up, and we felt pretty victorious. We made it through this night. We had just finished around eight o'clock, and my resident said, "Well, gee, that wasn't so bad"—meaning the whole hurricane. And then the lights flickered. And the hospital generators went out.

By the afternoon it was actually kind of sunny out. The streets had some debris in them from other buildings, but otherwise no major water. But the power was out, so we figured that we would probably start evacuating patients by ambulance that night or the following morning.

On Monday night there was a little bit of water in the gutters, as always in New Orleans after it rains. The city was completely dark. I barely slept. I just couldn't sleep with everything going on. And the AC was out, so now it's like 100 degrees inside the hospital.

When the sun came up on Tuesday morning, one of the nurses called me to the window, and we looked out and there was water around the hospital. And we suddenly realized we were in a much more dire scenario than we had ever imagined. Evacuating patients would not be done by ambulance. We knew immediately the levees had broken.

We thought, "Okay, now the actual rescue effort will have to come via boats." We also started having regular meetings. Every four hours we met in the lobby. The lobby was raised enough that we didn't actually get water.

We couldn't call floor to floor. We couldn't call anyone's local cell phone. We lost all contact with local families. Some of the nurses worked that entire week without knowing if their families were okay. But we did have long distance on landlines, so we would call our families who were farther away. I could talk to my family in Michigan, and they were frequently our source of communication.

Very early on Tuesday we made a rigorous system of getting patients out of the hospital—but that really relied on somebody coming to get us. We handwrote out their medical discharge summaries, which for a lot of patients was two or three pages, and we handwrote that out in triplicate. We put one copy of that with three days of medications in a plastic bag, and we pinned it to our patients' gowns. One of the problems was actually physically getting patients out. We knew that we would have to carry them downstairs, but we didn't have enough spine boards for all the patients in the hospital. You never have to use 450 spine boards at a time. So the janitors actually made them out of tables and doors. They were fantastic.

We had so many close calls in which we were told, "Yes, the National Guard is coming," or "FEMA is coming," and they're going to be rescuing us on boats. And we would get our patients all prepared, and we'd get the little things pinned on them. They were ready; we really felt like at this point medically they needed to go. By late Tuesday one of my patients was already two days out from missing dialysis, so we knew that it was very crucial. We had no idea that it was going to be four days of close calls.

Those close calls were really taxing on us emotionally and

physically because we would get the patients ready to go. We would get them psychologically prepared, we would get ourselves prepared, and then it wouldn't happen.

Wednesday we started to be concerned. I was much more concerned about water than I ever was about food because you can live a long time on very little food. But water was a big concern. It was so hot in the hospital that people were sweating so much. We started allotting a gallon a day for our patients for water. And I was very perplexed as to why we couldn't just have a little boat or a little helicopter zip in and drop off some water supplies. On Wednesday, Thursday, and Friday morning we had very small amounts of food for patients, subsistence level. Twelve hundred calories a day. They were getting things like cornflakes, or one night they got a half a cup of green beans and a roll. And I remembered being very apologetic with the patients that there was so little food.

Justin: How was their morale?

Kiersta: Unbelievable. So fantastic. I mean the patients were always joking. The patients I was really concerned about were the patients that were aphasic and couldn't talk to us. We pushed them to the window so that they could see the water, and we were constantly explaining what was going on to the best of our ability. I mean, I probably went around to every patient's room ten times a day to say, "Okay, this is what we know right now," 'cause I just wanted them to feel like they were in the loop.

On Tuesday we had this contest. People started hanging sheets out their windows with slogans on them. We said, "Okay, we're going to have our own banner." So we found markers and paints. I went around to every patient and asked them what our slogan should be for Five West. And finally the one we came up with was "Five West Got the Thunder, We're Not Going Under." It's not exactly grammatically correct, but the spirit was there. It was really like that was our way of trying to maintain our spirit. We spent a lot of time on our banner, hung it out the window. We could see other floors' banners. One of the banners was "Baby Katrina Born at 2:30 Last Night." Later on we found out the mother had waded through the water to have her baby.

But the patients were upbeat, and I was surprised at how little they complained. As the week went on, I think people felt a little more afraid. And on Thursday I really perceived that our patients felt that they might be left. We were listening to the radio, and we had heard rumors that in other hospitals doctors and nurses had just left patients behind. I don't even know how much of that is true, but I think our patients started to get concerned that things were bad enough that maybe people would take off. And so we spent a lot of time reassuring them that we would never leave, that we would stay until the very bitter end.

Justin: During the early part of the week I was in Baton Rouge, and I remember having conversations with you—I could reach you by landline—and I had the number for the floor. So we probably talked four or five times. On Tuesday I think we were all hopeful. You know, "The National Guard's coming." And on Wednesday I just remember very clearly having a conversation in which you described the smell of gas in the building. And it really freaked me out. There were buildings catching on fire all over New Orleans. There were major institutions going up in flames. And it just occurred to me, "My God, you got a thousand people in this building, including my wife."

Kiersta: Yeah. I have to say that for me that was probably the point at which I was most afraid. And a lot of things happened in the hospital: We had a sniper attack on Thursday. But I was never as afraid as I was on Wednesday. We smelled gas in the afternoon, and we could not figure out where it was coming from. First we thought maybe it was just from the water in the street 'cause you could see a slick of gasoline from cars. But we realized it was coming from inside of the building. And our maintenance guys were fantastic. They were looking to find the source of it, but it was dark. And I realized the building was so flammable; there's all this oxygen in here. I was walking up and down the stairs, and one of my patients' husbands, who is a lovely seventy-year-old gentleman, was walking up the stairs with a lighter. I said, "Oh my gosh, you have to put the lighter out." And he said, "Well, I don't have any other way to see my way around." So I said, "I'm going to give you my flashlight. You cannot light a lighter." But I realized there were a lot of people in the building that were probably using candles, lighters—and you get the sense that no help was coming to us. What are we going to do if there is a fire? Pick up the phone and call 911? It felt very hopeless. At that point I wrote this letter to you and to the rest of my family.

Justin: I know you had the opportunity to go back to Charity a few days ago for the very first time in nine months. You found the letter, which you left there on your desk.

Kiersta: I mean, I felt a little weird writing it, and it feels a little strange now because obviously we all survived and we were fine. But at the time I did have a feeling that something might happen. And I think I really tried to minimize what was going on in the hospital to you even though I did tell you about the gas leak. But this is the letter I wrote at 8:00 P.M. on Wednesday, August 31:

> A morbid thought to leave a letter like this and probably totally unnecessary and paranoid. But I'm hoping it will help me feel better, and maybe allow me to get a few winks tonight. I probably don't need to go into details. Let's just say that things have gone from bad to worse, and then into the next level of really bad. . . .
>
> What an amazing 37 years I've had. More love, adventure, and fun than most people have in a very long life. My favorite part has been the joy in being a daughter, sister, friend, and wife—and the rest never mattered much. I hope I squeezed a lot of life out of life, you know. I think I did. I still consider myself the luckiest person I know.
>
> Justin, you're the love of my life, sweetie. The thought of all my wonderful family and friends has been the thing that has gotten me through these trying times.
>
> Love, love, love, Kiersta

It's hard to read. You know, after I wrote that letter, I felt so much better. And also they fixed the gas leak. After that, I just felt very strong.

Justin: What did you think about me coming to the hospital?

Kiersta: I didn't think you should come to the hospital. But just suffice it to say you did come into the hospital through a lot of different channels, hitching a ride with someone to New Orleans and then getting on a boat with the New Orleans SWAT team and hitching your way into the hospital. And even though I was really not happy for you to come in 'cause I was worried about your safety, when you came in I was very happy to see you. You came in, and you had Snickers bars and peanut butter for our patients and water in a cooler. It was just great. It was like you were this hero.

Justin: I just remember the things I didn't bring. There was a lot of initial excitement over peanut butter and Snickers bars, and then it's like, "Where are the batteries? Where are the flashlights?" I was like, "Well . . . (*Laughter.*) I did my best."

Kiersta: You were there for the last day and a half, and you were really helpful. On Friday, when Louisiana Wildlife and Fisheries came to evacuate our patients on boats, you helped us carry them down the stairs, and you were exhausted by that point. We were carrying patients down the stairs, and they had everything pinned to them. We really didn't know where they were going.

It was probably the biggest leap of faith of my life to put these people I'd been caring for on boats. We knew they were probably going to go to the airport into other hospitals, but it was very emotional. Patients cried. I cried a lot in getting them on those boats, because it was like we were just putting them into the great unknown. Then after we got all the patients out, the boats kept coming. So all of the staff lined up in the halls, and it was like, "Wow, this is really happening. We're really getting out." They only took three, four, five people in each boat, and we suddenly realized we probably weren't all going to the same place. We had no idea where we were going. We've never all been together as a group again since Charity Hospital closed and everyone was laid off. We didn't know that at the time. We thought we would all be together again at some point, maybe pretty soon.

They took us to buses. Luckily, you and I were together. We did have some people from my floor and other people that I knew from the hospital. And it was on the one hand an incredibly jubilant atmosphere. The sun was setting, and the driver turned up the AC and turned up the music.

Justin: We had this fantastic music. And we were free. . . .

Kiersta: Our patients had all survived. It was amazing. But at the same time, you know, it was sad because for me it was the first time seeing the city submerged. Remember we drove over the I-10 overpass? When I saw the city submerged—and I could kind of, off in the distance, see our neighborhood and see it was submerged—I thought, "God, this is just the beginning." We all knew that we had a long road ahead of putting our lives back together, and ultimately that was going to be much harder than those six days we spent at Charity. I had that very distinct sense at that point, riding out on the bus, that my life was going to be about the "before and after." That it was going to be "before the hurricane" and "after the hurricane." And I wonder if when I'm ninety years old it's still going to be before and after. I think so. I think in some ways it will always be.

Justin: All those people—hundreds and hundreds of workers, who ended up losing their jobs, really put in a heroic effort.

Kiersta: Unbelievable. The janitors. The security guards. They made us feel like we could get through it with all the craziness going on around us. They allowed us to take care of patients—and no one has said thank you to them.

Justin: I'll never forget it. It was just incredible. And it was really an honor to see that and be a part of it.

May 27, 2006

THE STORY
OF STORYCORPS

When I was a kid growing up in New Haven, Connecticut, in the early 1970s, my parents had a cassette recorder and microphone around the house. One night when I was eleven years old, my grandfather, grandmother, and two of her sisters came to our apartment for a holiday dinner. My grandmother Rose Franzblau was a larger-than-life character. The oldest child of Eastern European Jewish immigrants, she raised her four younger sisters after they were orphaned during the flu epidemic of 1918. She graduated from college, earned a Ph.D. in psychology, and after World War II went to work as an advice columnist at the New York *Post* for more than a quarter century. I knew her as a small whirlwind of a lady who filled up every room she walked into. That afternoon in New Haven, I decided to set up the tape machine and record her.

When we were done, I brought in my grandfather and then my great-aunts. I remember I was a lousy interviewer—butting in incessantly with goofy comments—but I captured their voices nonetheless.

When I was thirteen years old, my grandmother passed away, and one by one over the next several years my two great-aunts and my grandfather died as well. At some point I went looking for the cassette of the interviews I'd recorded. It was nowhere to be found. Still today, more than twenty-five years later, when I go to my parents' house I search for this tape. I know it's gone, but just in case . . .

In 1988 I stumbled into radio completely by chance as a twenty-two-year-old headed to medical school. One afternoon, I was walking through New York City's East Village and a storefront caught my eye. It was a tiny sliver of a shop with imaginatively decorated windows. I went inside and saw that the store was empty except for the couple who ran it. They were excited to have a visitor and wanted to show me around. It was a store for addicts in recovery, with all sorts of 12-step books and self-help materials meticulously displayed. There was no mistaking the love and care that infused every inch of the cramped shop.

The couple, Angel Perez and his wife, Carmen, said they were recovering heroin addicts. They brought me to the back of the store and began telling me about their dream: to create a museum to addiction. Carmen had recently been diagnosed with HIV, and they were determined to see this museum rise before she passed away. They showed me scale models of the building, which they'd constructed out of tongue depressors and plywood. They had blueprints for every floor and intricate drawings of each exhibit.

They pulled out a loose-leaf binder thick with rejection letters from wealthy New Yorkers to whom they'd written for help. While it was clear that these were form letters, the Perezes didn't read them that way. Language as simple as "Congratulations on your idea" or "I wish you luck" gave them hope that the next request was going to lead to funding. All the while they were only weeks away from having to close their tiny storefront for lack of business.

I was moved by their courage and spirit, and I thought they deserved some attention. I went home, pulled out the Yellow Pages, and began calling all of the local TV stations to see if any of them might do a story. No interest. I flipped to the radio stations and called them as well. No interest whatsoever. At some point I dialed the number of a community station I'd never even heard of, WBAI. The news director at the time, Amy Goodman, took the call. She said it sounded like a great idea, but that they didn't have any reporters to cover it, so why didn't I do it myself? That afternoon I took a tape recorder and went back to see Angel and Carmen. I sat down beside them and began to record. From the moment they started speaking, I knew that I'd found what I wanted to do for the rest of my life.

Tape in hand, I went to WBAI and put the story together. It aired the next evening. Gary Covino, a producer from NPR in Washington, D.C., happened to be driving through New

York City and heard the piece. He called the station and picked it up for NPR's *All Things Considered*. I decided against medical school. My fate was sealed.

As a young radio producer I did piece after piece about ordinary Americans with extraordinary stories, focusing on underdogs in hidden corners of the country. I quickly learned about the power of radio, the capacity of people speaking from the heart to move listeners at the most visceral level; and I discovered how grateful subjects were to be heard and to have their stories told with dignity.

In 1993, I produced a radio documentary with two thirteen-year-old boys, best friends growing up on the South Side of Chicago. Lloyd Newman lived in the Ida B. Wells housing projects; LeAlan Jones in a house right next door. I gave them tape recorders and asked them to record a week in their lives—what it's like to grow up in one of the most dangerous and impoverished neighborhoods in the country. I spent a few hours training them to use the recording equipment, and then they were off.

LeAlan and Lloyd taped themselves at home and at school, getting into mischief around their neighborhood and taking bus adventures through downtown Chicago. They interviewed family, friends, and each other, and named their documentary "Ghetto Life 101."

Sitting in my room in Chicago, listening to a recording of LeAlan climbing into bed with his grandmother and asking her about her life, was an epiphany. It was one of the most intimate and powerful moments I'd ever heard; the tape all but

Lloyd Newman (l.) and LeAlan Jones (r.) in 1993

glowed with the love radiating from this conversation. The microphone had given LeAlan the license to ask questions he had never asked before—about the father he never knew, about his mother's mental illness, about his grandmother's childhood. The interview opened up lines of conversation between LeAlan and his grandmother that continued long after the taping ended. Years later, after LeAlan's grandmother died, these tapes became some of his most treasured possessions. "They're enough to sustain me for a lifetime," he said.

At about the same time I learned of a series of interviews from the 1930s and '40s housed at the American Folklife Center at the Library of Congress. Most of these were conducted as part of the Works Projects Administration's Federal Writers' Project by a small cadre of historians and folklorists. (Alan

Lomax; his father, John Lomax; and Zora Neale Hurston are the best known among them.) They drove throughout the country, lugging enormous acetate disk recorders in the trunks of their cars, to capture the stories and songs of everyday people.

On these recordings you can hear the voices of former slaves reflecting on their lives, prisoners in Mississippi's Parchman Penitentiary singing work songs, Harlem fishmongers hawking their wares, pool players in Washington, D.C., talking about the bombing of Pearl Harbor the day after the attacks. Many of these were perfectly recorded. I was mesmerized. Hearing these voices transported me back in time in a way that no photograph, movie, or book ever had. They struck me as historic artifacts beyond value. I wondered why nothing along the lines of these WPA interviews had been undertaken since—top-quality recordings of the voices of everyday Americans across the nation.

A few years later I produced a radio documentary about the last flophouses on the Bowery in New York City, where homeless men slept in prison-cell-size rooms covered in chicken wire for as little as five dollars a night. Later, the documentary was turned into a book of photographs and oral histories. I remember bringing early proofs of the book into a flophouse and sharing them with the residents. One of the men looked at his story, took it in his hands, and literally danced through the halls of the old hotel shouting, "I exist! I exist!" I was stunned. I realized as never before how many people among us feel completely invisible, believe their lives don't matter, and fear they'll someday be forgotten.

Out of these and a myriad of other experiences and influences, StoryCorps began taking shape in the summer of 2002. Having seen the positive impact that participating in documentary work could have on people's lives, I wanted to open the experience up to everyone. I hoped to create a project that was all about the act of interviewing loved ones, with only a secondary emphasis on the final edited product—in essence inverting the purpose of traditional documentary work from an artistic or educational project created for the benefit of an audience to a process principally focused on enhancing the lives of the participants.

From there it was a matter of figuring out the details. I knew the interviews should be between two people who cared about each other. I wanted there to be some kind of a helper present who could run the equipment and assist in the process. I thought the sessions should take place in an intimate space. I wanted the interviews captured with the highest standards of excellence—even better than the recordings you hear on the radio. I thought forty minutes was probably about the right length of time for each session, since I'd found that interviews can sometimes drag once they get close to an hour.

I wanted participants to get a copy of the interview, but I also wanted to make sure that the session would never get lost. I made a cold call to Peggy Bulger, Director of the American Folklife Center at the Library of Congress, home to the WPA interviews I so admired. I told Peggy what I was thinking and asked if the Folklife Center might consider housing the collection. Miraculously, she said yes. The ground was laid for StoryCorps.

In early 2003, a small team of colleagues and I started piloting the project. We rented a recording studio in Manhattan's Chinatown and built a simulated booth out of seven-foot-tall pieces of thick acoustic foam. I invited my great-uncle Sandy to record the first session. Sandy was eighty-eight years old at the time, the last living family member of my grandparents' generation. He had been married to my grandmother's sister Birdie for fifty-five years. She had passed away several months before the interview. Unlike Birdie and her sisters, my great-uncle Sandy was not an over-the-top character. I knew him as a gentle, quiet man with a dry sense of humor. I wasn't at all sure if the interview would work.

Uncle Sandy and I sat together in this mock booth, and for forty minutes he told me stories I'd never heard before. He talked about his first date with Birdie, how he'd asked her to meet him on a tenement stoop on Manhattan's Fourteenth Street. "I see this vision of purple coming down the street," he recalled. "She was so glamorous, and I thought, 'What the hell is she going to see in me, a two-bit farm boy?' That's when I tried to duck out. I turned and tried to get in the door. But it was locked. And I often think if that door was open, it would have ended there. It was the luckiest thing that ever happened to me." With that, he broke down weeping.

At the end of the session I asked him how it felt. "I hate to say this, but it's a good feeling," he said. "I don't have to act like I'm happy with everything—because I'm not. And I never will be." At eighty-eight, Sandy still drove around New York City in his car. I learned that he would listen to that CD of his interview over and over again on his drives. A good sign.

StoryCorps is, if nothing else, an experiment in human communication. Leading up to the opening, I had all sorts of concerns about whether we could actually pull it off. Would we get *Jerry Springer* moments—families zinging each other during sessions and breaking into screaming fights—or worse? Would people make reservations to use the booth as a personal recording studio and cut song demos? Would participants agree to sign the release at the end of the session so that the material could go to the Library of Congress? How would they feel about having the facilitator in the booth? Would the idea just flat-out fail?

Happily, from the day we opened in October 2003 it was clear that this little booth in the middle of Grand Central Terminal was something of a miracle.

The first thing we noticed were the tears, not unlike with my uncle Sandy. A facilitator told us about a husband and wife who came to reminisce about their lives. At some point in the interview the husband started to talk about his experiences liberating a concentration camp after World War II. He began to weep. Then he *really* started to cry. At the end of the session the wife told the facilitator that they'd been married for fifty years, but that this was the very first time she'd ever seen her husband cry. They both proclaimed their StoryCorps interview a wonderful experience.

At around the same time, an eighty-nine-year-old grandmother came to StoryCorps with her twenty-three-year-old grandson. She recorded a beautiful interview about growing up in immigrant Jewish New York, meeting her husband, her feelings for her children and grandchildren. At the end of the

session, the grandson asked, "Grandma, is there anything you want to tell me you've never told anyone before?" And the grandmother proceeded to tell her grandson that she had been molested by her uncle as a child. Nobody in the family had heard anything about this. The grandmother said it was a great relief to get it off her chest. She expressed no qualms about signing the release to place the interview in the Library of Congress. She was so proud of the session that she invited StoryCorps to her ninetieth birthday celebration to play excerpts for her family and friends.

Indeed, in the weeks after we opened, almost all of the participants signed the release for their interview to go to the Library of Congress. Since then, upward of 95 percent of StoryCorps participants have placed their interviews in this archive. Many people say that knowing their recording is safe for future generations is one of the most important elements of their StoryCorps experience. It makes sense. Since I fell in love with radio twenty years ago, I've come to believe that there's something of the soul captured in the human voice and that an audio recording is one of the most intimate and powerful records one can leave behind.

Because of the intimacy of the interviews and concerns about identity theft and privacy issues, from the earliest days of the project we were apprehensive about making the entire collection accessible to the general public. We decided initially not to put full interviews on the Web. (For the time being, researchers can go to the Library of Congress, show an ID, and listen to any session they choose.) Instead, we chose to edit a short excerpt from one interview each week on our Web site for all to hear. A handful of these were broadcast on public radio in New York and nationally on NPR. In May 2005, we began airing StoryCorps stories every Friday on NPR's *Morning Edition*, the top-rated morning radio show in the country, to an audience of more than 13 million listeners. Today, it's among the most popular features on public radio.

Other aspects of the project seemed to work equally well. The facilitators took to their jobs with skill and grace, their presence deeply valued by participants. Something about that third person in the booth seemed to keep the conversations flowing. Instead of saying, "I told you that story a million times!" and clamming up, cantankerous grandmothers would turn to the facilitator and launch into an old family yarn as if the facilitator were listening for the entire world. Facilitators started referring to this as "the magic of the booth."

From the day we opened, StoryCorps has worked relentlessly to reach out to underserved populations. We have recorded interview sessions with homeless people, the mentally ill, foster care kids, people with AIDS, and beyond. Early on, a homeless woman came to the booth to tell her story. (When a participant comes alone, the facilitator will ask the questions.) At the end of the session she insisted on giving the facilitator her food stamps as a contribution to the project. She wouldn't take no for an answer. Then she headed off to the bank so she could lock the CD of her interview in a safe-deposit box along with her most valuable possessions.

Part of the appeal of the "citizen interview" model of StoryCorps is that sessions can be conducted in any language the participants choose, as long as one person in the pair can communicate minimally with the facilitator. As soon as we opened, we began recording interviews in Spanish, Russian, Arabic, and Tibetan. At some point Chinatown's Cantonese community got word of StoryCorps, and it briefly became something of a fad there. We had days when everyone who came to the booth recorded their sessions in Cantonese—telling stories, laughing, crying. Most of the facilitators didn't have a clue what was being said, but they knew that the participants were having a ball.

Some people came back over and over again. A schoolteacher named Louisa Stephens made a reservation every few weeks to come to the Grand Central booth. Eventually, she recorded close to one hundred interviews with family, friends, students, or even people she met in the subway or walking down the street. One day early on, a facilitator asked what kept drawing her back to the booth. "I love it," she said. "I exercise restraint and discipline in not coming down here every couple of days. You come to the booth and the door shuts, and it is just so quiet. It feels like something in your brain opens up, and you can expose parts of yourself too fragile to expose to the noisy world. And you can engage each other in a way that you can't in ordinary life. It also makes me feel as if I'm speaking to people in the future—it gives me a toehold into another world. It's just *perfect*."

Not all the news in those early days was as encouraging. From the very start, we believed that StoryCorps should be accessible to everyone at little or no charge. Each interview costs us more than $250 to record, but we decided to ask for only $10 as a suggested donation to participate. If participants couldn't afford the $10, no problem; if they wanted to give more, great. We knew this business model gave new meaning to the term *nonprofit*, but were determined to make up the difference through donations and grants.

We had some early success with foundations, but before long the rejection letters started piling up. StoryCorps is an undertaking unlike anything attempted before, so it didn't fit in any foundation's guidelines. No funders seemed interested in taking a risk on this untested project. We watched our bank account dip each week. Before long we were perilously close to bankruptcy. I asked a close friend from college, now a banker, to take a look at our books and assess the situation. He said it could go either way: If we got an infusion of cash over the next few weeks, we might survive; otherwise, it was all over.

Fortunately, a few days later, some visionary philanthropists stepped in. The funding freeze-out ended. We've been expanding the organization ever since. Today, StoryCorps is one of the fastest-growing nonprofits in the nation.

A few months after we opened, a Brooklyn couple came to the Grand Central booth: Danny and Annie Perasa. He worked as a clerk at Off-Track Betting; she was a nurse. The two were consummate New York characters with storied lives and thick Brooklyn accents. They had come to the booth because they wanted to document their love affair. Danny recalled their first date twenty-five years before: "I said, 'I'm going to deliver a speech, and at the end you're going to want to go home. You represent a dirty four-letter word, and that word is *love*. If we're going anywhere, we're going down the aisle because I'm too tired, too sick, and too sore to do any other damn thing.' And she turned around and said, 'Of course I'll marry you.' "

On the table inside the booth sat a stack of love letters they'd brought with them.

> **Annie Perasa:** You write me a love letter every morning. If I don't have a note on the kitchen table, I

*Danny and
Annie Perasa*

think there's something wrong.

Danny Perasa: The only thing that could possibly be wrong is I couldn't find a silly pen.

Annie *(reading):* *"To my Princess: The weather out today is extremely rainy. I'll call you at 11:20 in the morning—"*

Danny: It's a romantic weather report. *(Laughs.)*

Annie: *"—and I love you, I love you, I love you."*

Danny: I always feel guilty when I say "I love you" to you, and I say it so often. It's like hearing a beautiful song from a busted old radio—and it's nice of you to keep the radio around the house. When a guy is happily married, no matter what happens at work, there's a shelter knowing that when you get home, you can hug somebody without them throwing you down the stairs and saying, "Get your hands off me!" Being married is like having a color television set—you never want to go back to black-and-white!

The moment we heard their voices, we fell head over heels for Danny and Annie. They embodied so much of what Story-

Corps was about—the eloquence, power, grace, and poetry in the words of everyday people; the notion that the lives of the people we pass walking down the street can be as compelling— even more compelling—than those of the rich and famous.

Danny and Annie fell in love with StoryCorps as well. They came back to the booth to read more love letters. Danny started bringing in characters he'd befriended over the years: a major-league umpire, an ambulance driver, a retired undercover narcotics detective (see page 83). Just about every week Danny would call the office to see if we wanted him or Annie to visit the booth. "I had a cataract operation over the weekend. Do you need me to come in and talk about it?"

Danny and Annie eventually became the unofficial spokespeople for StoryCorps, and we began traveling the country together, talking about the project at conferences and press events. Danny and Annie never ceased to astound me with their kindness, humor, wisdom, and, most of all, their boundless love for each other. Danny was not the type you'd necessarily peg for a great romantic; he was short, bald, nearly toothless, and cross-eyed. But Danny Perasa had more romance in his little pinkie than all of Hollywood's leading men put together.

In January 2006, Danny was diagnosed with end-stage pancreatic cancer. In February we renamed our Grand Central booth in honor of him and Annie. A week later, too sick to travel to the booth, Danny asked us to come to his house in Bay Ridge, Brooklyn, to record one last StoryCorps conversation with Annie:

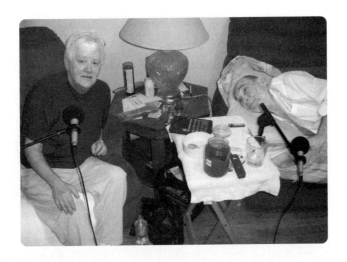

Annie and Danny recording at home

Annie: The illness is not hard on me—it's just the finality of it. And he goes along like a trooper.

Danny: Do you have the Valentine's Day letter?

Annie (*reading*): *"My dearest wife, this is a very special day. It is a day on which we share our love, which still grows after all these years. Now that love is being used by us to sustain us through these hard times. All my love, all my days and more. Happy Valentine's Day."* (*Crying.*)

Danny (*crying*): I could write on and on about her. She lights up the room in the morning when she tells me to put both hands on her shoulders so that she can support me. She lights up my life when she says to me at night, "Would you like a little ice cream?" or "Would you please drink more water?" Those aren't very romantic things to say, but they stir my heart.

In my mind and my heart there has never been, there is not now, and never will be another Annie.

We recorded this interview on a Thursday. It aired on *Morning Edition* the next Friday. Danny passed away two hours later. E-mails flooded into NPR's Web site. In all, Annie received close to fifteen hundred condolence letters from StoryCorps listeners.

At his funeral Annie carried a copy of these letters in her arms and placed them inside the casket to be buried with Danny. She kept a second copy at home. She continues to read one of these condolence letters each day instead of her daily love note from Danny.

AFTERWORD

Today StoryCorps is growing at a pace that I never could have imagined. Day by day, interview by interview, StoryCorps is having an impact on participants' lives—reminding them that they matter, that they have touched the lives of others, that they won't soon be forgotten.

It takes courage to walk into a StoryCorps booth. The conversations typically focus on mortality and love, two of the most difficult topics to tackle. But the rewards are clear, especially in the mail that arrives at our office each week.

This note came to us from Kay Spencer, who interviewed her father in Charleston, West Virginia:

> My dad's StoryCorps interview has taken on tremendous new significance for us. You see, we buried Dad last Wednes-

day. Needless to say, I'm still numb and probably in denial. I simply cannot comprehend that he's not coming back.

But let me tell you about the significance of our Story-Corps experience. Dad's illness and death happened so quickly that I had not had time to label the CDs and get them to my siblings. When Dad died, we decided to use part of the interview in his funeral. I had asked Dad about what he was proudest of in his life and how he wanted to be remembered. His answer both astounded me and humbled me. . . . His answer to both questions was "my six kids."

With that answer I saw him cry tears I had never seen. Then, at the end of the interview, I turned the tables on him, telling him all those special things I wanted to make certain he knew. Little did I know how very important those words would become.

We used the excerpts in the funeral, so all my siblings heard, in Dad's own voice, what was most important to him. And we all were able to smile, knowing he had heard what was most important to us as well. Then, at the end of the interview, Dad sang with me one of our favorite songs from childhood.

Last spring, when I first heard about StoryCorps, I knew it was something I wanted to do with Dad. Now, looking back, I cannot even put into words the gratitude I feel for the fact that this opportunity was there for us. There is more I could say, of course, but perhaps this will let you know at least a bit of the importance of StoryCorps for our family.

My entire family will forever be grateful.

Afterword

I hope that simply reading or listening to the Story-Corps stories can prove transformative as well. These interviews remind us that, contrary to what we might infer from the media, we are not just a nation of celebrity worship and consumption but, rather, a people defined by our character, courage, and heart. These stories are a record of our shared humanity. Hearing them, it becomes clear that no matter who we are or where we come from, there is much more in common that we share than that divides us. These stories are a reminder that if we spent a little less time listening to the racket of divisive radio and TV talk shows and a little more time listening to each other, we would be a better, more thoughtful, and more compassionate nation.

We've only just begun to tap the potential of StoryCorps. I hope that someday the project will become part of the fabric of American life, accessible to anyone who wants to participate. I hope it grows into an enduring American institution that documents and defines the character of this nation. And I hope that someday StoryCorps may even succeed in creating a change in our culture, shaking us out of a reality TV–induced slumber and redirecting our energy toward careful listening, honoring our elders, and embracing our neighbors.

Working on StoryCorps has been the most exciting and inspiring experience of my life. It has been a great privilege for the entire StoryCorps team to gather these first ten thousand interviews. We are now hard at work collecting the next ten thousand.

I invite each of you to record an interview and become part of the StoryCorps family. By listening closely to one another, we can help illuminate the true character of this nation— reminding us all just how precious each day can be and how truly great it is to be alive.

ACKNOWLEDGMENTS

StoryCorps exists today because of the sweat, love, and un-wavering commitment of hundreds upon hundreds of staff members, facilitators, part-timers, volunteers, partners, con-sultants, and funders. Many thanks to everyone who has had a hand in bringing this project to life.

My deepest thanks goes to the staff of StoryCorps—the hardest working, most dedicated and brilliant team one could ever hope to work with. The core staff in the early stages of the project included Karen Callahan, Steve Clair, Michael Hsu, Sarah Kramer, David Miller, Matthew Ozug, and David Reville. Those who have held leadership positions since in-clude Kayvon Bahramian, Heather Burke, Emily Feit, Lisa Jan-icki, Marion Kahan, Nora Levine, Edith Presler, Melvin Reeves, Tracy Serdjenian, and Nick Yulman. Our current and recent staff includes Ellen Baker, Carolyn Bancroft, Zachary Barr, Eliza Bettinger, Edith Bolton, Shana Bromberg, Jennifer Carr, Emily Carroll, Lizzy Cooper-Davis, Amanda Davis, John Edwards, Michael Garofalo, Jackie Goodrich, Jennifer Goya, Julia Guarneri, Maria-Mercedes Hubbard, Emily Janssen, Piya Kochhar, Katie McGowan, Morgan Monaco, Ryan Murdock, Veronica Ordaz, Dalton Rooney, Terry Scott, Katie Simon, Phoenix Soleil, Vanara Taing, and Dina Zempsky. Thanks also to each of the fifty-plus facilitators who have served a term with StoryCorps to date.

Special thanks to Operations Director Karen Callahan, who has worked tirelessly and brilliantly on behalf of the project since its inception; Founding Director David Reville, who did so much to bring the project to life; and StoryCorps Director Donna Galeno, whose heart, spirit, and talents have taken StoryCorps to new heights.

Our board of directors had the courage to green-light this adventure and have supported it ever since: Board Chair Woody Wickham, Michael Alcamo, Senator Bill Bradley, Brian Byrd, Gladys Chen, Dick Hecht, Truda Jewett, Deborah Leff, Jim Moore, Tom Moore, Jack Rosenthal, and Adele Silver.

Our original architecture and design team included Michael Shuman, Eric Liftin, David Reinfurt, and Jake Barton. Special thanks to Michael Shuman, who literally built each of our booths from the ground up. Thanks also to Jo Flattery, Debra Carey, Gillian Kocher, Joe DePlasco, and Matthew Traub at Dan Klores Communications.

Thanks to our first broadcast partner, WNYC's *The Brian Lehrer Show*. Gratitude also goes to the staff of the fifty-plus public radio stations that have partnered with us across the nation. There are far too many names to mention here, but everyone of you is a valued and beloved member of the Story-Corps family. It gives us enormous pride each day to be part of the public radio system. Thanks to our national broadcast partner, NPR's *Morning Edition*, with special thanks to Executive Producer Ellen McDonnell. Also at NPR, thanks to Bill Chappell, Micah Greenberg, Steve Inskeep, Jennifer Kinloch, Kevin Klose, Joyce MacDonald, Reneé Montagne, Andi Sporkin, Ken Stern, Maria Thomas, Blake Truitt, Jim Wildman, and especially Jay Kernis, who has been our champion throughout. Thanks to the Librarian of Congress, Dr. James Billington, and the staff of the American Folklife Center, especially Director Peggy Bulger and Joanne Rasi.

We appreciate Nancy Marshall and Dawn Banket for giving us our first home in Grand Central Terminal, and Mike Kaufman for introducing us to Danny and Annie Perasa. Thanks to Dickie Riegel and Larry Metz at Airstream for putting StoryCorps on the road. Our gratitude to everyone at the Lower Manhattan Development Corporation who helped with the creation of our Lower Manhattan Booth, with special thanks to Anthoula Katsimatides and the members of our 9/11 Family Advisory Board. We are honored to work with the World Trade Center Memorial Foundation, especially Joe Daniels, Alice Greenwald, and Jan Ramirez. Special thanks to Norene Sullivan, who has been instrumental in our 9/11 work.

Thanks to the MacArthur Foundation Fellows program for making it possible to dream up StoryCorps. Thank you to our first corporate sponsor, Saturn, and especially to our current corporate sponsor, AT&T. Thanks also to our major foundation funders, the Open Society Institute and the Ford Foundation. At OSI, thanks to Lori McGlinchey, Nancy Youman, and especially Gara LaMarche. At the Ford Foundation, thanks to Orlando Bagwell, Rosalie Mistades, and Annie Rhodes; gratitude also to the foundation's Good Neighbor Program. Thanks to Emily Giske, speaker Christine Quinn of the New York City Council, deputy mayor Kevin Sheekey, and New York City mayor Michael Bloomberg.

Deep appreciation to Larry Kaplen and the Kaplen Family Fund for their critical and timely support, and to Joe and Carol Reich for their visionary and generous support of our Memory Loss Initiative; gratitude also to Wendy Block.

Thanks to the Righteous Persons Foundation, the National Endowment for the Arts, the MacArthur Foundation General Program Fund, and the Marc Haas Foundation. Profound thanks to Stanley Shuman, who has been a great supporter, advocate, and advisor to this project.

We owe an enormous debt of gratitude to the Corporation for Public Broadcasting—Kathy Merritt, Erika Pulley-Hayes, Jacquie Gales Webb, Greg Schnirring, Michael Levy, Tim Isgitt, Vinnie Curren, and especially CPB president Pat Harrison. Profound thanks also to the CPB Board of Directors, with special thanks to Board Chair Cheryl Halpern. CPB has been our largest funder since day one of the project; StoryCorps simply would not exist without it.

Acknowledgments

Thanks to Latham & Watkins LLP, especially Jeanne Berges, Holland & Knight LLP, Tekserve, and all the others who have provided services and funding to propel this project forward.

For their wise and thoughtful counsel, gratitude to Barbara Becker, Paula Berezin, Nathaniel Deutsch, Beverly Donofrio, Gabi Fitz, Jennifer Gonnerman, Barbara Hall, Joe Katz, Chris Novack, Tom Tryforos, and Jason Wright. Special thanks to Dan Delany. For inspiration, thanks to Lonnie Bunch, Robert Coles, Bill Ferris, Barbara Kirshenblatt-Gimblett, Jack Tchen, Studs Terkel, and Steve Zeitlin.

Thank you to the StoryCorps staff who had a direct hand in creating this book: Sarah Kramer (who also serves as senior producer for StoryCorps), Michael Garofalo, Katie Simon, and especially Grant Fuller and Lizzie Jacobs. For manuscript suggestions, thanks to Kathrina Proscia. Harvey Wang offered valuable advice on photography. Thanks to our fact checker, Darren Reidy, and to the Tape Transcription Center in Boston.

Much of this work is about gifts between generations, and in creating this book I received a great gift from my mother, Jane Isay, who took a summer out of her life to read and cull through thousands of pages of StoryCorps transcripts. Helping to create this book was a fortieth birthday present to me. I'm not sure if she knew what she was getting into, but it's the best gift I ever received.

Thanks to our magnificent agent, David Black. At Penguin Press, our gratitude to Ann Godoff, as well as Tracy Locke, Laura Stickney, Maggie Sivon, Lisa Vitelli, and Amanda Dewey.

Thanks especially to our longtime editor, friend, and cheer-leader Scott Moyers, who believed in this project from the get–go.

Most of all, thanks to all the members of the StoryCorps family—participants and listeners—who give this project its life and meaning. This is only the beginning.

StoryCorps Facilitators, 2003–06

James Angelos

Kayvon Bahramian

Carolyn Bancroft

Zachary Barr

Eliza Bettinger

Mitra Bonshahi

Lisa Bradley

Michael Clines

Elaine Davenport

Karen DiMattia

Kamilah Duggins

Jonah Engle

Pat Estess

Emily Feit

Michael Garofalo

Anna Goldman

Jackie Goodrich

Shaleece Haas

Chris Heaney

Lisa Janicki

Emily Janssen

Piya Kochhar

Ian Koebner

Sarah K. Kramer

Susan Lee

Nora Levine

Justina Mejias

Nadja Middleton

Ryan Murdock

Brett Myers

Maddy Nussbaum

Veronica Ordaz

Roger Peltzman

Edith Presler

Nick Pumilia

Michael Ramberg

John Randolph

Jason Reynolds

R. Lena Richardson

Rani Shankar

Nelson Simon

Laura Spero

StoryCorps Facilitators

KIM STEVENS

MAISIE TIVNAN

ANDREW WILSON

ALEXANDRIA WRIGHT

NICHOLAS YULMAN

APPENDIX

Favorite StoryCorps Questions

- What was the happiest moment of your life? The saddest?
- Who was the most important person in your life?
- Who has been the biggest influence on your life? What lessons did this person teach you?
- Who has been the kindest to you in your life?
- What are the most important lessons you've learned?
- What is your earliest memory?
- What is your favorite memory of me?
- If you could hold on to one memory from your life for eternity, what would that be?
- Are there any words of wisdom you'd like to pass along to me?

- What are you proudest of in your life?
- How would you like to be remembered?
- Do you have any regrets?
- What does your future hold?
- Is there anything that you've never told me but want to tell me now?
- Is there something about me that you've always wanted to know but have never asked?
- Turn the tables: This is your chance to tell the person you're interviewing what you've learned from him or her and what that person means to you.

You can find more StoryCorps questions at www.story corps.net/. You can also find information on how to record an interview yourself.

StoryCorps is sponsored by AT&T.

Major funding for StoryCorps comes from the
Corporation for Public Broadcasting.

Other major funders include the Ford Foundation; the Marc Haas
Foundation; Hasbro's September 11th Children's Fund; the Kaplen
Foundation; the Lower Manhattan Development Corporation, which is
funded through Community Development Block Grants from the U.S.
Department of Housing and Urban Development; the MacArthur
Foundation; the Open Society Institute; Joe and Carol Reich; and a
September 11 Recovery Grant of the American Red Cross Liberty Fund.

Additional funders include the Carnegie Corporation of New York, the
J. M. Kaplan Fund, the National Endowment for the Arts, the New York
City Council, the New York City Department of Cultural Affairs, the New
York Community Trust, the New York State Council on the Arts, the
Righteous Persons Foundation, the Peter Jay Sharp Foundation, and
United States Artists.

StoryCorps was launched in 2003 with seed funding from the Carnegie
Corporation, the Corporation for Public Broadcasting, the MacArthur
Foundation, the Rockefeller Foundation, and the Steven H. and Alida
Brill Scheuer Foundation.

StoryCorps is a project of Sound Portraits Productions,
created in partnership wth NPR, the American Folklife
Center at the Library of Congress, and public radio stations nationwide.

Additional museum partners include the Smithsonian National Museum of
African American History and Culture and the World Trade Center
Memorial Museum.

Continue the Conversation

Visit *www.storycorps.net* to:

- Learn how to interview someone important to you.
- Listen to more stories; share them with others.
- Subscribe to our podcast.
- Find out how to bring StoryCorps to your community.
- Support StoryCorps and help us to continue in our mission.

One hundred percent of royalties from this book will be donated to StoryCorps, a not-for-profit project.